Hungarian Ai

By George Punka
Color By Don Greer

 **squadron/signal publications**

A pair of Bf 109Gs of 101/3 Fighter Squadron, Puma Fighter Group, Royal Hungarian Air Force, climb out on patrol over Hungary during 1944.

ISBN 0-89747-349-3

If you have any photographs of aircraft, armor, soldiers or ships of any nation, particularly wartime snapshots, why not share them with us and help make Squadron/Signal's books all the more interesting and complete in the future. Any photograph sent to us will be copied and the original returned. The donor will be fully credited for any photos used. Please send them to:

Squadron/Signal Publications, Inc.
1115 Crowley Drive
Carrollton, TX 75011-5010

軍用機、装甲車両、兵士、軍艦などの写真を所持しておられる方はいらっしゃいませんか？どの国のものでも結構です。作戦中に撮影されたものが特に良いのです。Squadron/Signal社の出版する刊行物において、このような写真は内容を一層充実し、興味深くすることができます。当方にお送り頂いた写真は、複写の後お返しいたします。出版物中に写真を使用した場合は、必ず提供者のお名前を明記させて頂きます。お写真は下記にご送付ください。

Squadron/Signal Publications, Inc.
1115 Crowley Drive
Carrollton, TX 75011-5010

Если у вас есть фотографии самолётов, вооружения, солдат или кораблей любой страны, особенно, снимки времён войны, поделитесь с нами и помогите сделать новые книги издательства Эскадрон/Сигнал еще интереснее. Мы переснимем ваши фотографии и вернем оригиналы. Имена приславших снимки будут сопровождать все опубликованные фотографии. Пожалуйста, присылайте фотографии по адресу:

Squadron/Signal Publications, Inc.
1115 Crowley Drive
Carrollton, TX 75011-5010

Photo Credits

Pál Bagossy	Tamás Bencsó
Bela Benkö	György Birkhoffer
Attila Bonhardt	Mihály Böjtös
Endre Czigány	Béla Csapó
Károly Faludi	Jose Fernandez
Archiv Franke	Archiv Fernandez
Pál Gombos	László Gyenes
László Jávor	Mihály Karátsonyi
László Kiss	VitézJános Suttay-Koppány
Dr. Volker Koos	Ferenc Kovács
Gusztáv Kunár	János Lasztóczy
Lajos Lászai	János Lejtényi
Imre Mészáros	Archiv Meurer
Imre Molnár	Árpád Nagy
Kornél Nagy	Tibor Nagymarosi
Peter Petrick	Tibor Sinka
Tibor Szij	Gusztév Susztáv
Dezsö Szentgyörgyi Jr.	Bill Szikszay
László Stahl	Pál Takács
Tibor Takátsy	Emil Terray
Ferenc Vásárhelyi	László Winkler
Kálmán Wittinger	Dr. Alfréd Zách
Hungarian Aero Museum, Canada	
Syula Sarhidai	Sándor Bandi

Dedication

This book would have been impossible without the assistance of my friend Ferenc Kovács, a noted Hungarian aviation researcher and collector.

Overleaf: A Bf 109G-6 starts its engine on the ramp of Veszprém airfield during 1944. At this time RHAF Bf 109s were active in intercepting USAAF bomber raids over Hungary.

Forward

Hungary is a small country located in the eastern portion of central Europe. Its history began with the Huns and the Magyars (Hungarians), who came from the steppes west of the Ural mountains. Saint Stephen, the first king of Hungary, founded a Christian state in 1001 AD, and made the nomad Hungarians, who had kept the rest of Europe in fear, settle down.

The centuries that followed did not bring peace to the small nation. The Tartars devastated the country in the 1200s, and two centuries later, the Hungarians went to war with the Turks. Hungarians became tough fighters because of the constant warfare, but their numbers dwindled. Subsequent kings invited the peoples of other nations to settle the sparsely populated areas of Hungary in order to provide a protective bastion for Western Europe against attacks from the east. Today, the descendants of these early immigrants and the original Magyars call themselves Hungarians.

Both the First and Second World Wars devastated Hungary, and the peace treaties that followed each war, were harsh on the losing nation. Between the two world wars, the slogan, "We were a nation of horsemen, but we will become a nation of flyers," motivated Hungary's youth. They wanted to fly and to live. Instead they were sent to kill or be killed.

For almost fifty years, while Hungary followed the path of Soviet style socialism, researching the military history of the country was forbidden. Even the official historical documents could not present an objective picture, only that approved by the state.

As a result of the changes in the political climate during 1989, a group of former Hungarian Second World War fighter pilots invited their former allies and adversaries to gather together for a reunion in the Fall of 1992. Former Soviet, American, German, Rumanian, English and Hungarian pilots met with each other in Budapest, the city above which they had fought and where many of their friends had been laid to rest almost half-a-century ago.

The history of Hungarian military flying has been the object of much research and numerous studies, but the Western world knows very little of this, since most published volumes are in Hungarian and few people outside Hungary speak the language. After the Second World War, many Royal Hungarian Air Force pilots resettled in other parts of the

Hungarian soldiers man a listening post on the Hungarian border searching for intruding aircraft. Later, the Royal Hungarian Air Force would use German and Hungarian-built radar sets to detect intruders. (Punka)

One of the main types of anti-aircraft weapons used by the Hungarian armed forces was the Bofors L40 40MM gun. It was effective against low flying targets. (Punka)

world. Some found new homes in countries they had fought against during war. Only one fighter aircraft that was flown by the Royal Hungarian Air Force, 101/III Fighter Group in April of 1945, survived the war. This Messerschmitt Me 109G-10, serial number 611943, is now preserved in the Air Museum in Chino, California.

I started to research the history of the Hungarian Air Force during the Second World War at the time when such studies were forbidden. Travel abroad was not permitted, my letters were opened, and my friends were questioned by the authorities. In the past few years; however, political changes in Hungary made the situation easier. During the last twenty years, I have made more than 3,000 flights and I am still flying. I have spent 1,000 hours in the air flying various aircraft and helicopters, along with an additional 300 hours in hot air balloons. The garden of our weekend cottage is cluttered with the wreckage of Second World War military aircraft, to my wife's great annoyance, and my photographic archives is growing steadily.

Without the help of former pilots, navigators, gunners, radiomen and mechanics, I would have achieved nothing. They gladly and unselfishly talked to me about their experiences and let me borrow their log-books and personal photographs.

These men never considered themselves as heroes. Heroes are always created by circumstances and by the succeeding generations. Yet, what can I say about the pilot who landed his aircraft on the snow-covered Russian steppe, disregarding the approaching enemy infantry, to rescue his comrade who had crash landed, or about the pilot who flew his Me 210 into a Soviet fighter's machine gun fire in order to protect his commanding officer, whose aircraft already had one engine on fire. After the war, these men could not fly or were forbidden to fly. The broken, yet proud look on their faces gave me the inspiration to write this book. I sincerely thank them.

Help from other researchers and colleagues made my work complete. I learned from them how to systemize and utilize to the maximum the source materials. A lot of their work and photographs are incorporated into this book. My thanks go to my Canadian-Hungarian friend, Stephen J. Bathy and his wife, Margaret, for the tiring task of translation. Thanks to my wife and daughter for the countless cups of black coffee, tolerating the clanging of the typewriter keys, serving cold drinks and strength-giving goulash soup and taking over my job of walking the dog.

3

Introduction

During the First World War, Hungary was a part of the Austro-Hungarian Monarchy and ended up on the loosing side. Her army disintegrated and her armaments were either taken over or destroyed by the victorious nations. In the Fall of 1919, after the failure of a short-lived Soviet-style republic, a new Hungarian National Army was organized under French supervision.

The Peace Treaty of Trianon, signed in 1920, cut Hungary into pieces. Two-thirds of her territory, containing more than 3.5 million Hungarians, was given to the newly formed nations surrounding her. All the treaty allowed, in the way of defense, was a mercenary army of 35,000 officers and men, having no heavy arms or up-to-date equipment. Conscription was abolished and the number of officers and non-commissioned officers was set. The same limitations also applied to armaments. The army was not allowed to have tanks, anti-aircraft batteries or an air force. The Grand Powers strictly enforced these rules.

The impoverished country had to pay compensation damages from the war and support the tens of thousands of Hungarian refugees arriving from the detached territories. Under these conditions, Hungary did not have the economic base to establish and maintain a military balance with neighboring countries in the Danube Basin.

The development of the armed forces started in secrecy after 1927, with equipment and arms being secretly purchased from abroad, because the treaty forbade the establishment of any type of war industry.

On 22 August 1938, an agreement was signed in the Yugoslavian town of Bled that declared Hungary's equal rights to arm herself. In return Budapest agreed not to reclaim any of the detached territories by force of arms. This was not difficult to adhere to, since the official policy of the Hungarian government was one of a peaceful rebuilding.

The creation of a modern armed force began during 1938. The new military organization envisioned the establishment of the following units by 1942:

25 infantry brigades (each consisting of two infantry regiments)
1 cavalry division 2 armored divisions 2 mountain brigades
1 frontier guard brigade
1 river gun-boat flotilla
28 air force brigades, comprising eighteen fighter and ten reconnaissance squadrons.

At the beginning, the Air Force bought mostly Italian-built aircraft, but from 1941 on, German-built aircraft became available in quaintly. To urgently address the shortage of personnel, and because the Air

This Fiat CR-32 of 1/1 *Ijász* (Archer) Fighter Squadron carries the three tone camouflage adopted during 1940. CR-32s were active in the fighting between Hungary and Slovakia during March of 1939. (Kovács)

Force was supposed to be equipped with mostly Italian aircraft, 100 officers and 100 non-commissioned officer candidates were sent to Grottaglie, Italy for training. Of these, sixty were slated for fighters, ninety for bombers and the remaining fifty for reconnaissance aircraft.

After Austria's *Anschluss* in 1938, Admiral Miklos Horthy, Hungary's Regent, traveled to Kiel, Germany at the invitation of Chancellor Adolf Hitler. At this meeting, Hitler informed Horthy about the planned military action against Czechoslovakia and appealed for Hungarian assistance. Horthy disregarded Hitler's request.

The modernization of Hungarian Armed Forces required not only the expansion its manpower but the purchase of modern military equipment. Hungarian buyers soon realized that they could depend less and less on the war industries of the nations they called allies. These partners were getting ready for war themselves and most of the aircraft that were available for export were obsolete.

Under the July 1938 expansion, plan and using twelve aircraft per squadron as a base, the Air Force was short seven long range and forty-nine short range reconnaissance aircraft, fourteen night bombers and thirty-three medium bombers.

On 11 September 1938, the Munich Agreement was signed by the four great powers, Great Britain, France, Germany and Italy. In it they addressed the interests of Poland and Hungary. This was followed by the first Vienna Arbitration on 2 November that gave Hungary back 11,927 square kilometers of the detached territories.

After Germany carved up what was left of Czechoslovakia in the Spring of 1939, and Slovakia declared her independence, Hungary

This camouflaged Savoia Marchetti SM-75 bomber carried the code, E 103, on the fuselage side in Black. The aircraft carries the early Royal Hungarian Air Force markings which consisted of Red, White and Green chevrons on the tail and wings. The bomber also carried a White mushroom marking under the cockpit. (Winkler)

recovered Carpatho-Ruthenia, establishing a common frontier with Poland. Hungary's move offended Slovakia and the Slovakian Air Force retaliated by bombing Hungarian cities on 24 March. The Royal Hungarian Air Force (RHAF) rose to the defense and Hungarian Fiat CR 32 fighters engaged Slovakian Avia B-534 fighters and Letov bombers. The Hungarians emerged the victors, shooting down three aircraft over Ungvár and six over Szobránc. RHAF bombers attacked the Slovakian airfield near Iglo without loss. To provide professional air force personnel, on 31 March 1939, the Royal Hungarian Miklos Horthy Aviation Academy was established at Kassa.

The most serious problem was a lack of aircraft. On 29 July 1939, the RHAF had a force of only 252 aircraft. A 300 million Lira Italian credit line, combined with less and less access to German armaments, led Hungary to turn to Italy as the major source of supply for the air force. In November of 1939, they ordered fifty Fiat CR 42 fighters and, in December, seventy Reggiane Re 2000 Falco I fighters. Field trials were also started with Caproni Ca 135bis bomber which led to a contract for thirty-six aircraft to be delivered during mid-1940. The fifty CR 42s were delivered during 1940 and the first of the Re 2000s were flown to Hungary in May of that year.

During the summer of 1940, the poor relations between Hungary and Rumania intensified. The RHAF was put on alert, in spite of the fact

A Caproni Ca 135 bomber on a Hungarian airfield with the bomb bay doors open. This aircraft was assigned to the *Boszorkány* (Witch) Squadron. (Punka)

This CR 42 carried a camouflage of Light Green and Brown over its original overall Gray. The aircraft code, V-234, was in Red and the cowling and tail were Yellow. This Fait was assigned to 2/4 Fighter Squadron stationed in southern Hungary during 1941. (Punka)

that the Ca 135s were not yet equipped with bomb aiming equipment or bomb racks. On 7 August, a Rumanian fighter attacked a Ca 135 over the Hungarian town of Debrecen. As a reprisal, a Hungarian short range reconnaissance aircraft, acting without official orders, bombed a Rumanian air field. Besides these air attacks, numerous border incidents took place on both sides. War between the two nations was averted by the Second Vienna Arbitration of 30 August, brokered with the help of Germany and Italy. As a result, Hungary regained Northern Transylvania, land that had belonged to the mother-country for centuries.

1941 started with the reorganization of many of the RHAF's squadrons. Several were disbanded and only three bomber squadrons were retained of the original ten. The short range reconnaissance squadrons were cut back from ten to six and one of the three long-range reconnaissance squadrons was disbanded. Under the reorganization, each squadrons complement of aircraft became uniform, each consisted of eighteen aircraft, nine to three primary aircraft and four to six trainers per squadron.

A line-up of Caproni Ca 135 bombers of 3/5 Bomber Squadron parked on a Hungarian airfield. The aircraft codes on the fuselage side were in Black. The Ca 135 was nicknamed *Béka* (Frog) in Hungarian service, partially because of its camouflage finish. (Kovács)

Combat

Yugoslavia

In March of 1941, Yugoslavia joined the German-led Three Power Pact in Vienna. The German general staff had already completed the preparations for the military campaign against Greece and wanted to use Yugoslavian territory in the Balkans to march into Greece. To put a stop to these plans, the strongly English sympathizing Yugoslavian army and the definitely anti-German Serbian intellects, with secret British support, carried out a bloodless coup d' etat overthrowing the government and sending Prince Paul, the head of state, into exile. The new Yugoslav government declared the Tri-Power Pact invalid.

Hitler was forced to change his plans for the Balkan campaign and gave orders, on 27 March, to draw up new campaign plan against Yugoslavia. As a result, Hungary found herself in a serious dilemma. Shortly before these events, she had signed a Treaty of Friendship and a Non-Aggression Pact with the now overthrown Yugoslav government. The validity of these treaties was seemingly lost, although the new Yugoslavian government did not view it that way.

The *Wehrmacht* was hoping to count on Hungary as an ally. Their main aim was the unopposed transit of German troops through Hungarian territory, although if the German army had to force its way through Hungary, the unprepared Hungarian armed forces could do nothing to stop them.

The British ambassador sent the following telegram to the Hungarian government on 2 April: The British Government will sever diplomatic relations with Hungary if the German army is permitted to move through Hungary. If Hungary, for any reason whatsoever (for example to protect the Hungarians living in Yugoslavia) joins forces with Germany, she can count on a declaration of war from Great Britain and her Allies."

Hungary concluded that the immediate danger, a conflict with the Germans, was the greater of the two evils and the German army was allowed to move across Hungary on 4 April 1941.

A number of Hungarian built WM 21 *Sólyom* (Hawk) short-range reconnaissance biplanes saw action during the fighting over Yugoslavia. This WM 21 was the seventh aircraft off the production line. The large windows in the lower fuselage gave the rear seat observer a good view downward on either side of the fuselage. (Punka)

Admiral Horthy, the Supreme Commander, wanted his army to advance only to the historical frontiers of the former Hungary (i.e. reoccupy the areas that were detached after the First World War).

On 6 April, the *Wehrmacht*, with her Italian and Bulgarian allies, began their offensive against Yugoslavia and Greece. The Hungarian armed forces were still being staged, when aircraft of the Yugoslav[an Air Force attacked the staging points in southern Hungary, without a declaration of war from Yugoslavia. Hungarian anti-aircraft fire brought down two of the attacking aircraft. During the fighting, a Yugoslavian pilot of Hungarian decent, escaped to Hungary with his Bristol Blenheim light bomber. Using the half-a-million Hungarians who were living in former Hungarian territories in Yugoslavia as a reason for action, the Royal Hungarian Armed Forces crossed the southern frontier during the early afternoon of 11 April.

Under the command of the Commanding Officer of the 1st Flight Brigade, the 1/1, 1/3, 1/4, 2/3, and 2/4 Fighter Squadrons, the 3/5, 4/3, 4/4 Bomber Squadrons and the III Short-Range Reconnaissance Squadron took part of the action against the Yugoslavian forces. The response from the Yugoslavian Air Force was weak because of poor weather conditions. On the morning of 12 April, Hungarian fighters were covering the concentration of ground forces, while three bomber squadrons were getting ready for action. But, because of the army units advance, only a few bombers actually carried out their bombing missions, the rest returned to their base. Meanwhile, the fighters were carrying out low-level attacks over enemy territory against truck columns and enemy trains deploying troops to the front. The short-range reconnaissance squadron was deployed, losing six of their out-dated aircraft, not to enemy action, but to mechanical problems. The campaign's most tragic accident happened on the Veszprém airfield, when the lead aircraft, a Savoia-Marchetti SM 75 (coded E-101), of the paratrooper battalion crashed on take-off due to a hydraulic-system malfunction. Among the casualties was the battalion commander, Major Árpád Bertalan.

On 13 April the military action against Yugoslavia ended and so did the first military action of the RHAF.

The Soviet Union

The Hungarian government had good relations with the Soviet Union, but these quickly deteriorated because of Hungary's action against Yugoslavia. Although Hungary did nothing different from what the Soviet Union had done with Poland in September of 1939 (this fact, however, was not considered by the Allies at the peace conference after the war).

The influence of the *Wehrmacht* over Hungary increased considerably after the Balkan campaign. It was also strengthened by a German sym-

Lieutenant László Kázárs CR-42 was damaged in combat and was repaired with patches that were done in the shape of White stars. The fuselage code was in Red and the fuselage band was in Yellow. (Punka)

Lieutenant László Kázár poses alongside his Fiat CR-42 of 2/3 Ricsi (Richie the dog) Fighter Squadron. He later went on to score two kills on the Russian Front during 1942. squadron. (Punka)

These Ca 135 bombers of 3/5 Bomber Squadron, during the Summer of 1941, carry the Yellow fusleage band assigned to aircraft operating on the Russian front. (Kovács)

pathizing Hungarian officer corps, the memory of the First World War alliance, and the fact that the Hungarian military committees could see, on three occasions, the success of the German military machine on the western European front. The Germans did not need Hungary's assistance for their Russian campaign because Hitler counted on a short, six to eight weeks, lightning war that he planned to accomplish using his own forces.

Another reason Hitler was not counting on the poorly equipped and mechanized Hungarian forces, was that he did not wish to get into arguments with his other ally, Rumania, whose relations with Hungary were still tense. In case of a victory, he was sure Hungary would have demanded the return of more of the detached territories.

On 4 June 1941, the Soviet government secretly inquired about Hungary's position in the case of a possible Russo-German conflict and indicated that the Soviet government would not be averse to Hungary's demand for further territorial claims against Rumania.

Two days later, at 1 pm the city of Kassa (now Kosice) was bombed by three aircraft of unknown type and nationality, which sported the yellow fuselage band and wing tips of the Axis forces (even today, the country of origin is unknown.) The raid left thirty dead and almost 300 wounded. The same day, a fighter with Soviet markings machine gunned an express train on Hungarian territory. The Hungarian government considered this action as "casus belli," and immediately declared war on the Soviet Union.

On the following day, at dawn, sixteen Junkers Ju-86K-2s of the 4/II Bomber Group (BG), eight Caproni Ca 135bis/U the 3/5 *Hüvelyk Matyi* (Tom Thumb) Bomber Squadron and several bombers from 4/1 *Isten Nyila* (God's Arrow) and *Isten Kardja* (God's Sword) Bomber Squadrons (which had been in readiness for days), accompanied by nine

The figure carrying a large ax on the nose of this Ca 135 of 3/5 Bomber Squadron was *Uz Bence* a Transsylvanian folk hero. (Punka)

Fiat CR 42 fighters carried out a bombing raid against Stanislav. The war had begun between the Soviet Union and Hungary.

The first Hungarian war dead of the conflict were flyers. On 29 June, A X. *Sólyomszem* (Hawkeye) Short Range Reconnaissance Squadron WM 21 *Sólyom* (coded F.242) did not return from a mission in the vicinity of Zielowa. Lieutenant István Sallay (pilot) and Captain László Bantyai (observer) were listed as missing in action. On the same day the first aerial victories were reported when Hungarian fighters shot down three of seven bombers attacking the town of Csap (Chop).

The main danger to the Hungarian fighters was crossing the Carpathian Mountains. In spite of it being Summer, the weather over the mountains was foggy and rainy. These adverse climactic conditions caused discomfort for the pilots, especially for recce pilots, who flew in open cockpit aircraft. Because crossing the Carpathians was not possible all of the time, aerial support for the advancing ground forces was not continuous. To provide more effective support, the 1/3 *Kör Ász* (Ace of Hearts) fighter squadron, commanded by Captain László Tomor, was deployed to the front in July of 1941. At the same time, the 2/3 *Ricsi* Fighter Squadron, the VII and X. Short Range Reconnaissance Squadrons were transferred to the airfield near Kolomea.

The Hungarian "Fast Corps", supported by a flight detachment, began operation on 9 July under the command of German Army Group South.

The I. and II. Short Range Reconnaissance Squadrons and the 1/3 Fighter Squadron were posted near the front line and on 12 July, 2/3 Fighter Squadron scored five kills over Soviet aircraft. Later that month the squadron was recalled to Hungary for a rest.

The fast advancing front required the rapid movement of air force units. By the end of June, twelve aircraft of the 1/3. Fighter Squadron were relocated to Sutyska, while the 1. *Holló* (Raven) and III. *Somogyi Bicska* (Pocketknife of Somogy) Short Range Reconnaissance Squadrons with nine Heinkel He-46 and nine WM 21s respectively were transferred to Bor.

The fighter and recce squadrons were moved forward again from Sutyska and their base was taken over by a "mixed' bomber squadron that was formed from 3/II. and 4/I. Bomber Groups with three Caproni Ca 135s and nine Junkers Ju-86s bombers. In early August, the Hungarian Air Force was supporting ground forces in the Savran - Pervomaysk Olviopol area. On 4 August, the fighters suffered their first loss when Lieutenant János Pettendy was declared missing in action.

On 6 August, six Caproni Ca 135s carried out attacks against targets in the Nikolayev area, their main objectives being the bridges. The bombers, under the command of 1st Lieutenant Szakonyi, destroyed the railroad station and scored direct hits on the bridge over the Bug River. (some 60,000 Soviet POWs were taken in this area). Szakonyi's aircraft

This Reggiane Re 2000 Héja carries the Hungarian insignia adopted in the Spring of 1942. The White cross was carried against a Black square and both the vertical and horizontal tail surfaces were marked with the national colors, Red/White/Green. On the vertical surfaces, the Red band was on the top, while on the horizontal surfaces the Red band was the inboard band. The aircraft also carried the squadron insignia of 1/1 Fighter Squadron which consisted of a Bumblebee on a circle and a Yellow identification band around the rear fuselage (Molnár)

(B.517) was hit in one of the engines and fell behind the rest of the group. It was attacked by six Polikarpov I-16s and in the engagement, the bomber's crew shot down three I-16s, and the remaining three gave up.

At the time of the battles around Uman, an experimental fighter squadron, equipped with seven Reggiane Re 2000 fighters, under the command of the Szolnok Fighter Squadron's commander, Captain László Gyenes, arrived at Sutyska to conduct a evaluation of the Re 2000 under combat conditions. Both fighter units were thrown into action on 11 August and accounted for five I-16s. The 1/3 Fighter Squadron flew 151 sorties and scored five victories within a month.

On 16 August, the VII Short Range Reconnaissance Squadron observed strong enemy troop movements on the road between Danzig and Doprienka. The squadron commander gave orders to equip nine WM 21 *Sólyoms,* with bomb racks capable of holding ten 10 kg bombs on each aircraft. The attack was successful, but five Hungarian aircraft were hit by heavy anti-aircraft fire.

On 26 August, the fighters claimed five more victories, followed by the destruction of ten more Soviet fighters over the Dniepropetrovsk bridgehead on the next day. The bombers were also active. Cornet Boór's aircraft scored a direct hit on the Bug River bridge and, as a result, the Soviet troops, still on the west bank of the river, were captured.

Five more victories were claimed by the fighter squadrons on 26 August. The flight detachment's aircraft flew a total of 555 combat sorties over enemy territory, carried out fifty-eight low-level attacks, dropped forty tons of bombs and scored twenty-seven kills for a loss of four aircraft between 7 July and 27 August.

The "Fast Corps" took over the defense of a section of the Dnieper River at the end of August. Besides being a part of this defense, the air force also supported the attack of the I. Armored Detachment that was pressing toward the Dniepropetrovsk bridgehead.

In early September, the I. Short Range Reconnaissance Squadron was recalled to Hungary. Since 13 July, the squadron had carried out seventy-two reconnaissance missions and eleven bombing attacks.

On 10 October, the 1/3.Fighter Squadron was moved forward to Dniepropetrovsk. Meanwhile, the weather started to deteriorate, with snow making the transfer of the squadron back to Hungary questionable. On 20 October; however, the weather cleared and the *Héjas* started their flight homeward, losing one aircraft over the Carpathian Mountains.

The III. Short Range Reconnaissance Squadron and the Mixed Bomber Squadron were still moving forward in Russia, although a short while later they too received orders to return to Hungary.

On 26 November, the fighters landed at the Mátyásfold airfield, near Budapest. During their four and half month tour of duty on the Eastern Front, they flew 447 sorties, achieved scored seventeen aerial victories and lost two aircraft and their pilots. With the return of III. Short Range Reconnaissance Squadron and the Mixed Bomber Squadron, the RHAF ended its first year of military activities.

A pair of Re 2000 of 1/1 Fighter Squadron on the Russian Front during 1942. Both aircraft have different fuselage positions for the national markings. The aircraft in the foreground has the marking applied father back than the aircraft in the background. Additionally, the fighter in the foreground does not have the Red/Green stripes painted on the vertical fin (only the White stripe innplace). (Molnár)

1942

1942 started out with the RHAF analyzing their operations of the previous year. While Hungarian flyers were better in close dog fights, their opponents had faster aircraft. The bombers were accurate at hitting their targets and the reconnaissance aircraft equaled their Soviet counterparts. The RHAF had learned a lot during the past year and the assumption was that the coming year would be similar to the previous one. The Red Army; however, started its counter-offensive in the Winter of 1941-42, changing everything.

By the Spring of 1942, it was determined by the German High Command that the Hungarian Armed Forces should be kept on the Eastern front. Therefore, the I. Flight Detachment was formed in early April.

Three Heinkel HE-111s of the first Independent Long Range Reconnaissance Group's l/l. Long Range Reconnaissance Squadron, under the command of Captain János Hollós, arrived at Konotop airfield on 12 June. Three days later, they moved on Amassovka. On 22 June, twelve Heinkel He 46s of the 3/2 Short Range Reconnaissance Squadron, commanded by Captain Zoltán Tròn, arrived and were immediately called into action, subordinate to the long range reconnaissance group. Two days later, eight Caproni Ca 135 bombers of the 4/l. *Boszorkány* (Witch) Bomber Squadron, 4th Bomber Group (BG) arrived at Konotop, commanded by Captain Andràs Inokai. Fighter defense was provided by eleven Reggiane Re 2000 fighters of the I/l. *Dongó* (Bumblebee) Fighter Squadron. This unit had begun operations in early July under the command of Major Kálmán Csukás. One of his squadron was 1st Lieutenant István Horthy, the son of Hungary's Regent.

The long-range reconnaissance group suffered its first loss on 2 July, when enemy fighters shot down a Heinkel He lll (coded F. 704). From 13 July on, the reconnaissance and fighter squadrons were continuously in the air. The deployment of the bombers was greatly limited due their poor mechanical condition. Escorting them was difficult too, because the Re 2000 fighters were much faster than the bombers. On 13 July, the bombers carried out four sorties against the Uryv bridgehead. Upon returning to base, three of the Ca 135s had to make forced landings and a fourth was missing. A day later, the fighter squadron was transferred to Stary Oskol, followed later by the bomber and reconnaissance units. Hungarian reconnaissance aircraft were kept busy for the rest of July.

The 2/l. *Keresztespòk* (Cross-spider) Fighter Squadron, equipped with eleven Hèjas arrived at the front on 30 July. On several occasions, in early August, the Ca 135 bombers were used to attack Soviet artillery

This Re 2000 *Héja* carries a Medium Green mottle camouflage over the Sand Brown base color. The fuselage code, V.4+21 was in Black. The aircraft was assigned to Lieutenant István Horthy, son of the Hungarian Regent, during the Summer of 1942 at Ilovszkoje in the Soviet Union. His personal marking which consisted of the logo *Sherif* in White script, flanked by two pistols and a White star was carried on the forward fuselage. (Punka)

positions and ground forces that were gathering on the east side of the Don River.

The Hungarian reconnaissance units were strengthened by the arrival of three Dornier Do 215B-4 bombers, transferred to the RHAF from Luftflotte 4. These aircraft were to serve alongside the unit's He-ll1Ps.

During one mission, a Heinkel He 111P-4 long range reconnaissance aircraft was flying toward Voronezh in excellent weather. Its mission was to cross the Don River and photograph the city of Voronezh. As it approached the target, all hell broke loose. Almost thirty anti-aircraft batteries were firing at the lone bomber. The He-111 cleared the anti-aircraft zone, when five Soviet fighters made their attack. The first of them pulled in directly behind the Heinkel, spoiling the radio/gunner's chance to fire because of the Heinkels vertical tail. What the Soviet pilot did not know was that this Heinkel was equipped with a fixed machine gun, housed in the fuselage under the rudder, operated by the radio/gunner, who opened fire. Seeing the bullets coming towards him, the Soviet pilot turned and gave the dorsal gunner a clear shot with his flexible gun. The Russian fighter went down, emitting first white then black smoke. The second fighter approached from the left, rear and used the same tactics as the previous pilot. The previous situation repeated itself when the radio/gunner and the photographer used the fixed and the flexible guns to fire on the fighter which was seen to burst into flames. The

A pair of Ca 135 bombers parked on a forward grass airfield on the Russian front during late 1943/ early 1943. The aircraft carry the Black and White cross marking, although they retain their original Italian camouflage with Yellow fuselage bands. Both aircraft have protective covers in place over their canopy glass. (Kovács)

This was the first Dornier Do 215B-4 long-range reconnaissance aircraft delivered to 1/1 Seven League Boots Squadron on the Russian front during 1942. The aircraft carries full Yellow theater markings on the fuselage and under the wings. (Molnár)

The windows on the lower fuselage of this Hungarian Ca 135 bomber were for the belly gun position. These Caproni's were in action bombing the Don River crossings being used by Soviet troops. By this time, it was becoming obvious that the Ca 135 was no longer suited for duty over the front. (Kovács)

mechanic/gunner, who was lying in the gondola, saw the third Russian fighter coming in to attack from below. He let it come in close and, as the Red-starred fighter opened fire from about fifty meters, he emptied the contents of an entire ammunition drum into the Russian aircraft, shooting it down. The remaining two fighters broke off the action. This particular aircraft, under the command of 1st Lieutenant Antal Kelemen, shot down a total of seven Russian aircraft.

On 4 August, Soviet troops crossed the Don River and the battle for Uryv began. Ca 135 bombers bombed troops crossing the river and the enemy force, beginning at dawn on 6 August, started a non-stop bombing campaign of Hungarian positions along the river. Although the *Héjas* could not prevent the Russian bombers attacking the area north of Uryv, a flight of two *Héjas* shot down two attacking Soviet fighters. The airfield occupied by JG 77 was heavily damaged by Soviet bombers, but the Germans reported several being shot down by Luftwaffe fighters.

On 7 August, a Soviet Il-2 shot down Cadet-Sergeant Péterffy's *Héja* over the eastern bend of the Don River. The fighter's wing was severe and the it crashed into Hungarian held territory. That afternoon, Hungarian Re 2000s attacked three German He 111s, which were bombing Hungarian lines by mistake. Major Csukás shot one of them down, thinking the Germans were Russian aircraft. Russian fighters were also engaged in dog fights over the bridgehead and a Hungarian He 111 of the long-range reconnaissance squadron was attacked by Russian fighters, shooting down three of the attackers.

On 9 August, a He-46 of the Short Range Reconnaissance Squadron shot down a Russian aircraft, while Hungarian fighters scored two kills. One aircraft of the 3/2 Short Range Reconnaissance Squadron was attacked by two Soviet fighters while covering the front lines, one was chased away by a Hungarian fighter and the second was shot down by the reconnaissance aircraft. Another reconnaissance aircraft managed to get away from Soviet fighters by flying into anti-aircraft fire causing the Russians to break off their attack.

Hungarian fighters found themselves facing twelve Russian fighters, which the first *Héja* flight had thought were Germans and flew on. The fighters shot down two of the Soviets, although Lieutenant Takács suffered thigh and shoulder fractures and was forced to make an emergency landing behind the front lines.

On 11 August, a Ca 135 of the 4th BG shot down an attacking Russian LaGG-3 fighter over Petropavlovsk during an attack on a Russian artillery battery.

Three days later, a Hungarian Long Range Reconnaissance He 111 crew shot down one of the fighters attacking it and claimed a second fighter as a "probable." In the fight, the Heinkel suffered heavy damage and had to belly-land upon returning to base.

On 14 August, an order arrived to destroy the bridge at Uryv. Three Ca 135s took-off, each carrying eight 100 kg bombs and eight 50 kg bombs. The plan was to drop the bomb loads simultaneously in anticipation of heavy anti-aircraft fire. Above Ilovskoye four Héjas joined them to act as escort. The Group Commander, Major Mocsáry, commanded the bombers with the Chief of Staff of the Air Brigade, Lieutenant Colonel János Németh, flying in the lead aircraft. The flight consisted of B.549, the lead aircraft, B.551 flown by Captain Schiller on the right wing and B.560, flown by Cornet Asztalos on the left wing . The flight approached the target at 8,200 feet (2,500 meters) where the cloud cover was three-tenths, with the cloud base at 7,800 feet (2,400 meters). The bombs were dropped at 1400, but, because the clouds partly obscured the target area, the lead aircraft released only half of its bomb load. A second run was made when the target became visible, but this time the lead bomber was hit in the right wing root by Soviet flak. The bomber burst into flames and started to dive toward the ground. Only Lieutenant Colonel Németh and the observer, 1st Lieutenant Orbán managed to bail out, the rest of the crew perished. The remaining two bombers completed their second run and scored direct hits on the bridge.

At dawn on 20 August 1942, 1st Lieutenant István Horthy (Deputy Regent of Hungary) crashed with his Re 2000 *Héja* shortly after takeoff. V.421 hit the ground near Ilovskoye and burst into flames. The circumstances of his death were subject to much speculation, even today. Many had suggested German sabotage (Horthy's sympathy for the English was well known), others still believe it was a pilot error in that he simply turned too sharply at low altitude and stalled.

On 23 August, a Ca 135 bomber was hit by heavy Soviet anti-aircraft fire but managed to get home on one engine. One of the fighters also fell victim to Soviet flak. The pilot, Sergeant Gyimes, bailed out and was captured by the Russians. During this period, Russian bombers were continuously attacking Hungarian airfields from a high altitude, while they did not inflict much damage, they did keep every one's nerves on edge.

As of 29 August the bomber unit reported that there was only one out of their nine aircraft flyable, due to mechanical problems.

On 9 September, the bomber group dispatched two flights to attack Uryv. They dropped their loads from 7,800 feet (2400 meters) and, while they came under fire from four Soviet anti-aircraft positions, none were hit. The second sortie of the day was carried out at 0720, and a third was launched at 0940. This time the target was Soviet infantry gathering in the forest outside of the village of Otychyha. A combined bombing and reconnaissance sortie against Hill 195.6 took place at 1704. All total that day the squadron carried out thirty sorties and dropped thirty-six tons of bombs.

The 1/1 Long Range Reconnaissance Group, was down to three flyable aircraft and received reinforcements in the form of three He 111s and four Do 215B-4 long range reconnaissance aircraft from Luftflotte 4.

By 25 September, the 1st Flight Detachment reached its twenty-fifth aerial victory. The long and short range reconnaissance squadrons had claimed twelve and three victories respectively, while the bombers claimed one and the fighters recorded nine kills.

German and Hungarian forces fighting at the Don River gained a

This Junkers Ju 88D of the Long Range Reconnaissance Squadron carried the fuselage code F9 + 15. The F and the first two digits were in Red while the last number was in Black. (Molnár)

breather when the Soviet High Command concentrated their forces at Stalingrad.

The Hungarian long-range reconnaissance aircraft were transferred to Kharkov-Osnava, while a flight of bomber crews was flown to Poltava to be retrained on He 111's. The first few fighter pilots were getting acquainted with the Bf 109F's.

The 3/2 Short Range Reconnaissance Squadron's aircraft were worn out beyond hope. The crews had fought with their obsolete He 46s for four months with only one being lost. The last sortie for the bombers ended in tragedy, when B 560, commanded by Cornet Asztalos received a direct flak hit and blew up over Kopanishche. The tragedy brought the 4/1 Bomb Squadron's 1942 operations to a close.

The fighter units claimed four victories in October and another in November. In November, the 5/2 Fighter Squadron and 5/1 Fighter Group staff were sent to the front to relieve the units posted there.

December was spent mostly flying reconnaissance missions and training flights and the long range units received their first Junkers Ju 88D aircraft.

The end of the year found the bulk of the Hungarian Flight Brigade in the vicinity of Ilovskoye.

1943

The Destruction of the 2nd Hungarian Army

The Soviet High Command had prepared a plan for a general offensive in the Voronezh area as early as November of 1942. The Red Army broke through at Stalingrad on the lines that were held by the Rumanian army, therefore the Soviet High Command hoped, and based on the reconnaissance report ,quite justifiably, that the resistance of the Italian and Hungarian allies would not be as stiff as the Germans. On 12 January 1943, the Red Army started its attack along a 155 mile (250 km) wide front against the 2nd Hungarian and the 8th Italian armies. By 18 January only a few pockets of Hungarian army resistance were observed along the Don River. The beaten Hungarian army retreated in an disorganized manner leaving their armament and equipment behind. Ten days after the start of the offensive, the 2nd Hungarian Army ceased to exist. A few detachments were holding out, including air force units who established a circular defense at Ilovskoye. They held up the Soviet troops long enough to get the heavily loaded transports and long range reconnaissance aircraft out of the encirclement. After blowing up all unflyable aircraft, the group broke out from the encirclement under the

Three old Junkers Ju 87A Stukas were given to the RHAF by the Luftwaffe to be used a trainers for crews that would be flying later variants of the Stuka on the Russian Front. These aircraft were based at Veszprém airbase during the Summer of 1943. (Bencsó)

This JU 87B-2 carries a three tone camouflage finish. The aircraft has had its weapons removed and was used solely to train aircrews for the Ju 87D equipped squadrons. (Punka)

A flight of four Ju 87D-5 Stukas return from a mission over the Russian Front during 1943. The aircraft have the wheel pants removed because they had a tendency to clog up with mud on the primitive airfields on the Russian front. (Stahl)

leadership of the legendary "Old Puma", Captain Aladár Heppes. They managed to take out all their wounded and weapons, although fifty percent of their aircraft were lost.

On 2 February, the reorganization of the Hungarian Air Force units on the Russian front began. The long range reconnaissance squadron continued operations, the fighter squadron was placed under the command of I/JG52, and the 4/1 Bomber Squadron was retrained on Junkers Ju 88s in Poltava. The intensification of the fighting along the entire front was indicated by the fact that the *Hétmérföldes Csizma* (Seven League Boot) Long Range Reconnaissance Squadron lost four aircraft during February. The 1/1 Fighter Squadron's Me 109F fighters were now tasked with supporting German Army Group South beginning on 22 February onward. Also during February, 5/2. Fighter Squadron began conversion training on the Me 109G's.

While Axis forces were preparing for Operation CITADEL in the Kursk area set for the Spring of 1943, Soviet forces were not wasting their time either. The Hungarian Long Range Reconnaissance

This Bü-131 (I.4+44) of the 1 Courier Squadron was camouflaged in a pattern of Gray/Brown/Green on the uppersurfaces with Light Blue on the undersurfaces. The unit marking was a chess piece. (Nagy)

Squadron's, which by now reached their 400th sortie reported, "At places where we could count 100 to 120 aircraft a day . . . now the number of aircraft has increased to an average of 900."

On 19 May, the 4/4 Bomber Squadron (later redesignated as 102/1) started operations from Kharkov. Also during this period, the Short Range Reconnaissance Squadrons were re-equipped with a new type of aircraft. Twelve Focke Wulf FW 189s, or as the Hungarians nicknamed them **Bel Ami** were delivered for 3/1 **Táltos** Short Range Reconnaissance Squadron. 2/2 **Kókuszdió** (Coconut) Bomber Squadron (which was later redesignated 102/2) completed conversion training on the Junkers Ju 87D and declared combat ready. During the Kursk Battle, Hungarian fighters claimed several victories and the short and long range reconnaissance aircraft were deployed as bombers.

Due to the rapid Soviet advance, 5/1 Fighter Group was relocated from Kharkov to Poltava during early September and a number of pilots were sent back to Hungary. From the remaining pilots, the 5/2 **Káró Ász** (Ace of Diamonds) Independent Fighter Squadron was formed. Later it was redesignated as 102/1 Fighter Squadron under the command of Captain Gyula Horváth.

Between May and November, the fighters had carried out 1,560 sorties and lost nine pilots. The Focke Wulf Fw 189 Short Range Reconnaissance Squadron, under Captain Imre Telbisz, carried out about 1,100 sorties by December, losing two aircraft in combat.

The 102/1 and 102/2 Bomber Squadrons, flying Junkers Ju 87Ds and Ju 88As, also reached the 1,000 mission mark. Several of their aircraft, mostly Ju 88s were shot down.

By the end of 1943, the Hungarian units were transferred to the rear for retraining and to re-equip. Experienced pilots were either transferred to training units or sent on furlough. There was relative quiet on the Russo-Hungarian front. The Long Range Reconnaissance Squadron's returned to their base in Hungary after handing over their surviving aircraft to the Germans.

At the beginning of 1944, the newly retrained, but inexperienced crews (especially in the Hungarian fighter units) played only a secondary role on the Eastern front. They escorted bombers, flew cover over the front, and rarely carried out independent fighter sorties. Another active squadron was the short range reconnaissance squadron which, under the command of Captain József Frauenhoffer, carried out many bombing missions and nuisance flights with their twin-boomed Fw 189s.

In March, the newly manned Hungarian Ju 87 Stuka squadron received twelve new aircraft, but because of the length of time required for conversion training, they did not get to the front before the end of January. Once they were declared combat ready, they were posted to III/SG 77 at the Polish front. Their number of sorties increased rapidly, but the number of encounters with Russian fighters also dramatically increased.

On 25 July, one Hungarian flight was taking part in an attack when

The 5/1 Puma Fighter Squadron received a number of Bf 109F-4B fighter-bombers equiped with DB 605 engines on the Russian Front during. The unit was tasked with supporting German Army Group South during early 1943. (Punka)

Captain (later Major) Aladár Heppes climbs into the cockpit of his Messerschmit Bf 109F-4B at Poltava airfield. The aircraft carried the fuselage code V.0 + 39. Captain Heppes led the successful breakout of air force personnel from the Soviet encirclement at Ilovskoye. The was known to his men as the "Old Puma." (Punka)

they met several P-51 Mustangs that were part of Operation FRANTIC III. The pilots of the American 307th Fighter Squadron, seeing the Stukas diving on their targets, quickly moved to intercept. One of the young Americans, Lieutenant Shipman, shot down one of the dive bombers. He then encountered several other Stukas and when he tried to get behind them, one turned into him for a head-on attack. The surprised American barely avoided a mid-air collision. Shipman attacked another Ju-87 but the gunner scored hits on Shipman's Mustang. After returning to base, Lieutenant Shipman reported that the Stukas carried White crosses on a Black square on the wings. These were the markings of the RHAFs Stukas and it was probably the Stuka piloted by Lieutenant József Bouczek, the flight leader. His gunner was Lance-Sergeant Zsélyi. Lieutenant Shipman was shot down by mistake by a P-38 Lightning over Budapest on 30 July and became a POW,

The Stuka squadron carried out 242 sorties by the end August and lost three Ju 87s and two aircrew. Earlier, in October of 19 43, the Germans had decorated all the Hungarian Stuka crews with the Iron Cross Second Class. The Hungarian Ju 87 unit remained in action on the Russian front in the Krakko (Poland) area till the end of August, 1944, when they were recalled to Hungary for conversion training on the Fw-190F fighter-bomber.

To strengthen the fighter force, a new Bf 109G squadron, 102/2

Although it carries proper national markings on the wings and fuselage, this Hungarian Junkers Ju 88C-6 heavy fighter has no fuselage codes. The aircraft was based on a forward field on the Russian Front during 1943. (Punka)

Fighter Squadron, was sent to the Eastern front. In a short time they had achieved several victories; however, the crumbling situation on the Russian front forced them to retreat further and further to the west.

102/l. Squadron shot down two Ilyushin I1-2s in the vicinity of Dukla on 14 September. On the next day they shot down a Yak-9 and a Il-2, loosing two of their own fighters and a pilot. During this period, the Experimental Fast Bomber Squadron arrived at the front, equipped with Messerschmitt Me 210Ca-l fighters. After a few training/combat missions, the squadron was moved back to Hungary.

The short range reconnaissance units turned over their aircraft to the Germans after being retrained on Bf 109 photo-reconnaissance aircraft; however, they no longer flew preplanned missions.

The bombers had their last effective combat mission on 2 June 1944. The target was Soviet troop concentrations and armored units disembarking from a train near Kivierce in Poland. Four Ju 88s took-off under the command of Squadron Leader Imre Homér. They had carried out a similar mission the day before without difficulty; however, on this mission they were greeted by heavy anti-aircraft fire. Russian fighters, ignoring their own flak, attacked the Hungarian bombers. On the return flight, two of the bombers were lost to Soviet fighters and one was damaged. After this mission, the unit, without their bombers, returned to Hungary for conversion to Fw 190s.

The fighter squadrons fighting on the Russian front were disbanded and reorganized into the III Group of the 101 Home Defense Fighter Wing. Hungarian operations on the eastern front were finished. From October of 1944 on, the so called Eastern Front was on Hungarian soil.

Hungarian ground crewmen work on a arrived Ju 88A-4 that has only a potion of its fuselage code applied. Often conditions at the front made it impossible to repaint aircraft with their proper markings. There were even times when Hungarian units flew their aircraft in the original German markings, retaining them until there was a lull in the fighting. (Punka)

RHAF Over Hungary

During the early part of the war, Home Air Defense was represented by anti-aircraft batteries and a few second-line fighter squadrons, since the war was far from Hungary. After Budapest was bombed by a Soviet night attack in September of 1942, the 5/1 *Bagoly* (Owl) Night Fighter Squadron (NFS) was established. The first aircraft used by the squadron were Fiat CR 42s, which were replaced by Re 2000 **Hèjas**.

By the end of 1943, the Soviet Union had the capability to reach deep into Axis countries. Additionally, the western Allies were continuously attacking German military targets and it became obvious that the possibility of Hungary being bombed depended only on the plans of the Allied High Command. The development of Home Defense fighter units became an urgent priority.

Bombers of the 15th Air Force, USAAF were steadily flying over Hungary from their Italian bases, but because the Hungarian government was secretly discussing peace with the Allies, and did not want to jeopardize the negotiations, it was forbidden to intercept the bombers. The reason for "no action" was not given to the units, therefore, they were understandably puzzled by the orders to stand down.

Hungary began producing Daimler Benz engines at the Danube Aircraft Factory near the end of 1942 and, in early 1943, production of the Bf 109G and the Me 210Ca-1 was begun. Re 2000s were also in production, together with the Ju 52 transports and several reconnaissance and trainer aircraft.

Because of the developing fighter program, it was now practical to re-equip the fighter squadrons with the Bf 109G. The first squadron to be re-equipped was the 2/1 Fighter Squadron near Budapest, it was followed by the 1/1 Fighter Squadron at Szolnok.

The 5/1 *Bagoly* NFS, under the command of Captain Ádàm Krudy, was re-equipped with Me 210Ca-1s, becoming combat ready in 1944. The Air Force Experimental Institute's defense, under the command of Lieutenant Colonel Lóránd Dóczy, was formed from the Institute's pilots and radiomen. This special destroyer squadron was equipped with twelve Me 210Ca-1s. This made a total of four squadron with which to combat the American bombers and their fighter escorts. The first combat occurred on 17 March 1944, and was one sided. Hungarian units failed to down any of the Allied aircraft and lost two Bf 109Gs to American fighters.

Budapest was bombed in a large raid on 3 April, the target being the Danube Aircraft Factory and its airfield. The factory's test pilots took part in the interception the intruders. A lone Me-210 was ordered by ground control to attack a bomber formation approaching from the south. 1st Lieutenant Kornél Nagy and his gunner, István Kuti, attacked the bombers but their aircraft was shot down by P-38

Early in the war, home defense of Hungarian territory was entrusted to light, such as this 40MM Bofors unit, and heavy anti-aircraft units and second line fighters. As the war progressed these units were reinforced and by the time the war ended, more than 300 American aircraft had been destroyed. (Punka)

Lightnings. Nagy was badly wounded, loosing an eye, and Kuti was killed. Two Bf 109Gs were also shot down by American escort fighters.

On 12 and 13 April, the 15th Air Force carried out several bombing raids against Hungarian cities. The Americans lost seven B-24 Liberators, six P-38 Lightnings and two P-47 Thunderbolts. Hungarian squadrons lost a number of Me 210s, and it became clear that the Me 210 could not hold its own against American escort fighters.

The 1/1 and 2/l Fighter Squadrons carried out 114 missions during April, scoring six kills for a loss of six pilots killed and one wounded. On 1 May 1944, the 2/1, 1/1 and the 5/3 (reserve) Fighter Squadrons

This Fiat CR 42, coded V2 + 11 was assigned to the 5/1 *Bagoly* Experimental Night Fighter Squadron during the Summer of 1943. The unit was tasked with the protection of Budapest from night attacks. Later, night fighter protection was furnished by radar equipped Bf 110s. (Punka)

The Héja II was built in Hungary by MAVAG under license with a WM 14 radial engine, Gebauer machine guns and a modified cowling. Many of these saw service in second line units on home defense duties. (Birkhoffer)

Aircrews are briefed by their unit commander in front of five Re 2000s Héjas. As the war progressed, units rotated back from the Russian front were retained at home for home defense. (Gách)

were reorganized into the 101/1, 101/2 and 101/3 Fighter Squadrons. This new **Puma Fighter Group** was under the command of Major Aladár Heppes. The **Pumas** baptism of fire came on 24 May when thirteen Bf 109Gs of the 101/1 Fighter Squadron shot down three B-24s, two P-51s and one B-17. Eight Hungarian aircraft were damaged and one pilot was lost. May saw little action, but five of the previous victories were confirmed.

The next large scale bombing by the Allies was on 2 June. The nearness of the front lines on the Eastern Front now made it possible for Allied aircraft operating from Italy to bomb targets in Germany and Hungary they land in the Soviet Union. General Eaker, Commander in Chief of the Mediterranean Air Command, took part in the first "shuttle" mission. The targets for the 15th Air Force's six-hundred bombers were the rail stations and the military garrisons at Szeged, Szolnok, Debrecen, Miskloc, Kolozsvár and Nagyvárad. The Allies lost ten aircraft on this mission.

On 14 June, 600 bombers entered Hungarian air space. The formation was attacked by thirty-two fighters from the 101 Fighter Group and by eighty German Bf 109s and Fw 190s. This force shot down a total of twenty Allied aircraft, while the Hungarians lost three aircraft and one pilot. The defenders; however, could not prevent the destruction of the nitrogen factory at Pet and the oil refinery at Ujszász.

Seven days later Hungarian pilots suffered a "black day" in their operations against Allied bombers. Twenty-eight flyable fighters from three squadrons, together with the Germans, attacked 658 bombers and 290 escort fighters in the Simontornya-Tihany-Tapolca triangle. The intercepting force lost a total of thirteen fighters with five pilots being killed. The Allies lost five P-38s and one P-47. Late in the month additional Allied attacks were carried out. On 26 June, No 205 Bomber Group (BG), Royal Air Force attacked Budapest with nearly 130 bombers. Most of the damage was done to the cities perimeter and the Manfred Weiss armament factory. The anti-aircraft defenses reported shooting down seven bombers. On the same day, an American bomber and fighter formation, some 550 strong, was attacked by thirty Hungarian fighters. Three bombers and two escort fighters were shot down, while the defenders lost three pilots. On the next day, the **Pumas** shot down three bombers and one Mustang, while the anti-aircraft units claimed a further nineteen aircraft. On 30 June, Hungarian and German fighters managed to break up several bomber formations and achieved four victories, losing one pilot in the process.

July was not any easier, with the air defenses becoming embattled from the beginning of the month. On 2 July, a devastating raid was launched on Budapest. Eighteen flyable Bf 109Gs of the 101 FG and 150 destroyers and fighters of the 8th German Home Defense Division rose to meet the more than 700 intruders. During this raid, the American

air force suffered its greatest loss over Hungary. The latest research indicates that at least fifty aircraft were brought down. The Hungarian Air Command confirmed five B-24s, one B-17 and one P-51 for the 101 FG, but did not confirm seven other claimed victories. Three Hungarian pilots lost their lives that day. One of the then unconfirmed victories

Bf 109Gs of the Puma Group fought both American and Soviet aircraft over Hungary. The aircraft in the background V.8 + 06 has the White fuselage cross overpainted white with Gray to make them less of a aiming point for allied gunners. (Karátsonyi)

Two pilots, Lieutenant Pászthy and Lieutenant Kovács, rest in the grass next to a Bf 109G while their ground crews prepare the aircraft for the next mission during the Summer of 1944. The unit's base was known as the *Puma Szállás* (Puma Camp). (Karátsonyi)

A ground crewman rests on the cowling of a Bf 109G-2 of 5/1 Puma Fighter Squadron. The aircraft carries the standard squadron marking, a Red Puma's head on a White circle, on the cowling.. (Punka)

over a P-51 was confirmed decades later. It was awarded to Cornet Leó Krizsevszky. The P-51 in question was flown by the American ace, Lieutenant Ralph K. Hofer, who crashed outside the Hungarian border.

On 3 July, the bombers that were attacking Arad and Szeged lost two Liberators and an additional four bombers were shot down by Hungarian fighters the next day. 7 July saw almost 1,000 bombers attack "oil targets" in Austria and Poland. The 101 FG intercepted the formation and shot down six Liberators, one Flying Fortress and three Lightnings. The Allies lost a total of twenty aircraft that day in the skies over Hungary. Hungarian fighters did not suffer any losses in the air but, on the ground, sixty-two were killed when an American bomber formation, on its return flight from Vienna, made a surprise attack on Veszprém airfield, dropping some nine hundred 33 pound (15 kg) anti-personal bombs. In the Pét - Hajmáskér - Balatonfüzfö triangle twenty-six American aircraft were shot down on 14 July. The rest of the month was relatively quiet, with Hungarian fighters claiming one P-38 shot down.

Nearly 800 aircraft of the 15th AF attacked Budapest in ten waves on 27 July. Hungarian and German formations intercepted them in the Lake Balaton and Székesfehérvár area and shot down twenty-nine bombers and fighters. Hungarian units were credited with four B-24s and two P-51s.

7 August brought more losses to the Hungarians. Eighteen aircraft of the 101 FS were escorting German destroyers southwest of Lake Balaton. An American P-51 formation, returning from Poland, attacked the formation and shot down eight Hungarian and German aircraft in a short engagement. Two of the Hungarian pilots were killed. One, Lieutenant László Molnár, was Hungary's top ace at the time with twenty-three kills. A third pilot was seriously wounded.

Between 20 and 30 August, the American Air Force bombed the airfields lying to the East of the Danube River. Their aim was to help the Red Army's budding offensive in the Iasi-Kyshynov area. Although they lost 10 aircraft, they did considerable damage to the installations. The Hungarian 102 Fast Bomber Squadron's twelve Me 210Ca-1s were destroyed on their home field at Hajduböszörmény, while the Luftwaffe lost some 120 aircraft of different types on the airfields at Berettyóújfalu

and Debrecen.

On 22 August, the 101 *Puma* FG reported its 100th victory achieved during the defense of the home land. On the same day, German-Hungarian force reported shooting down five Liberators. Throughout August, American bombing attacks continued against the railway stations and airfields at larger Hungarian cities. By the end of August, the Mediterranean Air Command had achieved total air superiority over Hungary.

The air attacks continued into September. On 12 September, the target again was Budapest. The capital was attacked by 856 bombers and at the same time, nearly 140 bombers and their escort fighters attacked the industrial district of Diósgyör on their return 'shuttle' from Poltava in the Soviet Union.

The American XV Fighter Command, formed from seven fighter wings, started operations during mid-September. Their activities were concentrated against railroad junctions in Trans-Danubia (that part of Hungary which lies west of the Danube River). In the second half of September, the Soviets began systematic aerial attacks against Hungary. In response, the 1st Air Division HQ ordered the establishment of the 101 Fighter Wing. Two of its fighter groups were the already fighting, the 101/I and 101/II Fighter Groups, while the first two squadrons of the 101/III were formed from the crews of the 102 Fighter Group's squadrons that were brought home from the eastern front. The third squadron was formed in December from pilots who returned from Germany, where they had been ferrying aircraft from the factories to the fronts.

This Luftwaffe Bf 110 of the ABKZ unit was stationed in Hungary to train Hungarian night fighter and fast bomber crews. The unit was based at Ferihegy during 1944. (Petrick)

This Wellington of No 205 Squadron, RAF was shot down during a night attack on Budapest on 3/4 April 1944. The aircraft crashed into Lake Balaton, killing the pilot, Sergeant Gordon Pemberton. (Punka)

On 6 October, the 2nd Ukrainian Army started its offensive at Debrecen, Hungary. The ground forces were supported by Colonel-General Goryunov's 5th Air Force which consisted of two ground attack corps, one fighter corps and one bomber division, for a total of nearly 1,100 combat aircraft. On the first three days of the offensive they flew 1,313 sorties and reported shooting down thirty aircraft. The task assigned to the Hungarian 101/I Fighter Wing was the protection of the defending ground forces in the Csongrád - Szeged area.

On both 9 and 10 October, the American XV Fighter Command attacked the Börgönd airfield where the Luftwaffe based a large number of Fw 190s, Ju 87s, Ju 88s, Ju 188s, and Ju 52s. The damage from the raid was extremely heavy, with a large number of aircraft either heavily damaged or, like some of the Hungarian Ju 87s stationed there, burned.

Hungarian fighters of the 101/I FG were returning home from the Makó - Szeged area when they were surprised by Mustangs on 12 October. Although short on fuel and ammunition, the Messerschmitts engaged the P-51s. In the ensuing fight, the 101/I Fighter Squadron claimed two P-51s, although the 2nd and 3rd squadrons were not as successful, they lost three aircraft and two pilots. After the fight the Mustangs attacked several airfields, destroying a number of Bf 109s and two Ju 52s.

The next day, the Americans repeated their visit and another ten Hungarian Ju 52s and two Fw 58s were destroyed. Their victory; however, was not cheap as the day before, with one B-24, one P-38 and one P-51 being shot down. The following day a total of eleven B-24s and B-17s were lost along with a P-38 and a P-51. The anti-aircraft units claimed a Mosquito and a Wellington bomber from No 205 Bomb Group, RAF.

The Allies lost another two P-38s on 14 October and, on both 17 and 18 October, the 101/1 and 102/2 Fast Bomber Squadrons, bombed the Soviet river crossings. On 20 October, the Me 210s attacked Soviet

The wreckage of a Junkers Ju 86, Bristol Blenheim and Focke Wulf FW 58 litter the ramp of the Flying Research Institute after a bombing attack against the field in April of 1944. (Punka)

This B-24H Liberator (Serial 4252380) of the 55th Bomb Wing, 406th Bomb Group, USAAF, made a forced landed bombing Budapest on 13 April 1944. (Punka)

front line positions and the next day enemy forward airfields were struck. During October, the Hungarian units flew one mission against American formations, while flying some twenty missions against the advancing Soviet

During action against the Soviets the Hungarians lost one fighter on 1 November, one on 2 November and two more on 4 November, including the leader of the 3rd Squadron. The fast bombers attacked Soviet truck columns carrying reinforcements south of Budapest. During the mission the Messerschmitts were jumped by Yak-9 fighters as they were pulling out from their dives. Two of the Me 210s were damaged and had to make forced landings.

On 5 November, 500 four-engine bombers, escorted by 198 P-51s and 139 P 38s attacked the oil refineries at Vienna/Florisdorf in Austria. On their return flight the bombers flew over Hungary, where they were intercepted by twenty Hungarian fighters. Over Lake Balaton, Mustangs of the 4th FG, 334th Fighter Squadron spotted six Bf 109s chasing a flight of Liberators. Four of the Mustangs attacked and the Hungarians broke away to the left and right. Lieutenant Zachman, accompanied by his wing man, Lieutenant Hudson, followed one Bf 109G. The P-51s set the Bf 109G ablaze and Lieutenant Zachman turned away and caught up with the bombers. That was the last time he saw his wing man, who was still following the burning Bf 109. Later he tried to contact Hudson on the radio, but there was no answer.

The pilot of the Hungarian fighter, Sergeant Pál Domján, later filled in the rest of the story. While trying to escape, he looked back and saw a P-51 flying along side him, with the American pilot pointing toward his tail. He looked hack and saw that the 109 was in flames. He jettisoned the canopy and bailed out. His Messerschmitt, now out of control, turned sharply and smashed into the Mustang. The Hungarian pilot was not aware of this until after he landed and the two aircraft crashed near one another. Lieutenant Horace S. Hudson died in the crash of his P-51, QP-X, serial 42-103570) shortly before 1300 on 5 November 1944. His opponent, Sgt. Domján, died on 2 January 1945, when his fighter was hit by Soviet flak.

Although they shot down four Liberators and one Mustang, the Hungarians lost four pilots. On the nest day, due to a oxygen system malfunction, the leader of the 4th squadron was killed when his fighter dove into the ground. His wing man, who was following him through the cloud layer, was also killed when he did not pull up in time.

The 101 Home Defense Wing ceased operations against the Anglo-American formations on 7 November. From that date on, they were sent on sorties solely against the Red Air Force. The reason for this tactic was that the strength and number of the Soviet formations had strongly increased in the area. On 8 November the 102/l Ground Attack Squadron (GAS) received the first of sixteen Fw 190F-8 fighter bombers. Its first action against Soviet armor took place on 16 November under the command of Captain Gyözö Lévay.

Between 13 and 16 November, the fast bombers were again attacking the enemy reinforcements and troop concentration points. A day later the 102/1 GAS carried out three sorties east of Budapest, where they attacked the Soviet flak positions. Me 210s blew up an ammo train

Captain Bodó (right) walks away from his Me 210Ca-1 on the airfield at Hajdúböszörmény. The 102/2 Fast Bomber Squadron was based here for attacks against Russian targets behind the Carpatian mountains. (Punka)

south of the capital.

On 19 November, the US XV Fighter Command attacked the road and rail lines in Veszprem County, including airfields and German - Hungarian troop movements. The next day, the ground attack squadrons were renamed fighter-bomber squadrons. Two days later, they were deployed together with the fast bombers south of Budapest. During the afternoon, six aircraft of the 102/2. Fast Bomber Squadron (FBS) were attacked by Soviet fighters with two bombers being shot down and two others heavily damaged.

The 101 Fighter Wing was thrown into action against the Americans eight times in November. and they shot down twelve Allied aircraft. They flew twenty-two sorties against the Red Air Force, claiming twenty-one victories. During this period the wing lost eleven pilots killed, five wounded and two missing.

By December, 102 Fast Bomber Squadron and 102 Fighter Bomber Squadron were relocated, with the fighter bomber group having only one combat ready squadron. Its second squadron was still being trained in Oels, Poland, under the command of Captain Homèr. On 4 December the weather halted most missions although the fighter-bombers attacked enemy troop concentration south of Lake Balaton. During their take-off the Fw 190s were attacked by Rumanian Messerschmitts and one was shot down. Four days later the squadron was forced to relocate because of the frequent Soviet bombing attacks.

On 9 December, the Fw 190s claimed a victory, but they also lost one of their own. A few days later they lost another three aircraft, two had been sabotaged and crashed on take-off, while the third one flipped over while attempting an emergency landing

On the 20 December, the l02/l FBS carried out four sorties over the front lines, losing one aircraft to flak. The fast bombers attacked truck columns north of Budapest. Two days later, four Hungarian fighter-bombers were flying cover for SG 2's tank busting Stukas when they were attacked by Ilyushin Il-2s and La-5s. The Hungarians shot down two of the Soviet fighters

23 December saw the formation of the 101 Night Fighter Squadron, equipped with Me 110G-4s, under the command of Captain János Hollós. The squadron flew several sorties without result. As the aerial battles continued, the number of victories over Soviet ground attack and fighter aircraft grew, but the constant fighting, relocating and bad weather also caused a number of losses for the defenders. Again and again fighters and ground attack aircraft flew over the encircled capital city, Budapest, together with Ju 52 transports. At night, German gliders made precision landings carrying ammunition and food for the defenders. The Hungarian l02/l. Transport Squadron, under the command of Captain Antal Bànhidy, took an active part in bring in these provisions.

Christmas Day saw the l0l/4 Fighter Squadron active in escorting Me 210s north of Budapest, where Soviet armor was reported to be advancing. After the sortie the 101/I. and 10l/II. FGs were moved from Veszprèm airfield to Kenyeri.

During the first eleven days of Soviet encirclement of Budapest, Soviet Air Forces flew 8,490 sorties and reported twenty-nine victories.

During the same time period, Hungarian fighters flew 291 sorties and achieved sixteen confirmed victories.

The fighter wing flew 1,414 sorties during 1944, they shot down 161 aircraft, while their casualties were forty-two pilots killed and nineteen wounded. Out of the 400 Bf 109s they received during the year, only eighty were still air worthy. The Hungarian Armed Forces lost more than sixty percent of their fighting force during the last four months of the year. In the defense of Budapest, between 21 December and 11 February, three entire divisions were ground up. By the end of 1944, the Red Army had conquered two thirds of Hungary. The three Ukrainian Army Groups had some one million troops, not counting the Rumanian and Bulgarian divisions under Soviet control. The German - Hungarian forces numbered half a million, with 240 thousand being Germans.

The German - Hungarian air force became active again during January of 1945. During the first five days of the month, they shot down four enemy aircraft. Me 210s and the Fw 190s attacked the advancing Russian infantry whenever they could. On 6 January, the command of Hungarian fighter units was turned over to JG 76 and, on 8 January, the 102 FBS flew its 2,000th sortie. The 101/8 FS flew a mission on 14 January over Csepel Island, shooting down two Soviet A-20 Bostons, two Lavochkin La-5s and one La-7. Two days later Hungarian fighters shot down three Soviet fighters and one bomber between Budapest and Lake Balaton. The fighter-bombers attacked one of the railroad stations in Budapest where Russian armor was being unloaded. Because of the

Lieutenant Bogati poses in front of his Fw 190F-8 fighter-bomber. The aircraft carried a crude White 60 code number painted on the engine cowling. The aircraft was armed with an AB bomb on the underfuselage bomb rack. (Bogáti)

heavy flak, the attackers dove almost vertically and after releasing their bombs pulled up between the buildings on either side of the streets. On the same day, the 102/2.F-BS received a number of new Fw 190s. They were flown to a front line airfield on 17 January and went immediately into action. During the following days, the 102 Fast Bomber and the 102 Fighter Bomber Groups attacked the roads heading south and west from Budapest in spite of a heavy snow fall and drifts.

On 18 January, the 6th German Army made a renewed attempt to reach the besieged capital. Four panzer divisions rolled easterly from the Várpalota area, toward the Danube and turned north when they reached the river. By 26 January, they were 18 to 20 km from Budapest. On 22 January, the 5th and 17th Soviet Air Forces flew 1,034 sorties. During this same time period, Hungarian fighters scored six more victories. The Fw 190s bombed enemy troop concentrations around Martonvásár and the formation commander's aircraft was hit by flak and went down. A total of two aircraft did not return from this mission.

The Germans were unable to break through the ring around Budapest and had to pull back to avoid encirclement by advancing Soviet forces. By the end of January, the last of the airfields in the besieged capital fell, making it impossible to further supply the city by air. Foul weather kept the Hungarian planes on the ground, but during the short sunny breaks, the Hungarians shot down another three Russian aircraft and lost one of their own. During this period, the 101 Fighter Wing received twenty-three new Bf 109G-10s to replace their losses.

On 11 February, the defenders of Budapest made a move to break out of the city. The Russians discovered the plan and massacred the concentrated troops with "Stalin Organ" rocket fire. Out the 44,000 men involved in the attempt, only 785 made it through the ring. Hungarian fighters were in action south of the capital, where they shot down thirteen Soviet aircraft but lost eight Me-l09s.

1 March saw the weather break and two flights of the 7th Squadron intercepted American bombers returning from Vienna and shot one down, which made a forced landing in Soviet territory.

The German 6th Army and the 6th SS Panzer Army started a large scale offensive in the area between Lake Velencei and Lake Balaton on 6 March, this was to be the last German offensive in Hungary.

On 8 March the 101/I and 101/II. FGs engaged Soviet formations and shot down one Il-2 and one Yak-9, for a loss of one fighter. Two days later, another four Il-2s and seven La-5s were shot down. The 13th of March saw the loss of four Hungarian fighters, although two Yak-9s and two Il-2 were shot down.

The 102 F-BG's aircraft were jumped by P-51s on 15 March, and four of the Hungarian fighter-bombers and their pilots were lost. By 18 March, Red Army troops were close to the Hungarian fighter-bomber's base, and aircraft taking-off went into battle right over their own airfield. The group was forced to evacuate their base and on the following day they returned to bomb their former base together with the surrounding area.

The Pumas clashed with the Soviet fighters on 20 March and the fighter-bombers lost two aircraft in combat, mainly due to the fact that the pilots were inexperienced and under trained. Up to 22 March, the 101. Fighter Wing had destroyed seven Yak-9s, five Yak-3s, five Il-2s, one A-20 Boston, one La-5 and one La-7 for a loss of two of their own. That day, American fighters made a low level attack at Vaszar, destroying seven Ju 52s and one Bücker Bü 131 on the ground, while a FN 58 was shot down on take-off. In the afternoon the Soviets attacked the airfield at Pápa. The bombers destroyed ten to fifteen aircraft on the ground and after the attack, the evacuation of the airfield began. Four tri-motor Fiat C-l2 transports of the 102/2 Transport Squadron were flown to Nagycenk (where they were blown up a short time later). A day later the l01/I and 101/III fighters flew to Szombathely, damaging and writing off many of their aircraft on the bomb catered air field.

On 26 March, the rest bomber group pulled back to Parndorf, Austria. The 101/III FS took-off from Grosspetersdorf, Austria on 27 March to

The half German/half Hungarian markings on this Bf 109G-2 indicates that it was probably one of the first aircraft to come off the Hungarian production lines. (Punka)

attack the rapidly advancing Russians. Three days later the fighter wing was moved to Wiener Neustadt, Austria. On the first day of April, Hungarian fighter and fighter-bombers carried out a series of low level attacks against the Russians advancing on Austria. Three days later Hungary fell to the Russians (4 April 1945).

A day later, after a front line reconnaissance mission, the Hungarian fighter wing was pulled beck to Raffelding. This was their last base before the war ended.

The fighter-bombers were attacking advancing Russian armor in southern Vienna, when they attacked by Il-2s. In the ensuing dog fight, the Hungarians shot five of the Soviet attack aircraft.

On 7 April, four Fw l90F-8s of the l02/l Squadron were attacked by P-51s. One Hungarian Fw 190 went down in flames, while the rest of the fighter-bombers, most of them damaged, tried to escape. The formation leader's aircraft was fired upon by the anti-aircraft defenses of Wiener Neustadt airfield by mistake. The pilot bailed out, but his parachute did not open fully and he was seriously hurt on landing. A wounded pilot tried to belly land his Fw 190 at the airfield, but miscalculated his landing, slid into an earth covered air raid shelter and blew up.

Two days later, the *Pumas* fought with Yak-9s over Vienna, with no results. The Group was then moved Sankt-Pölten and ten took-off at 1900 for a sortie, three of them returned damaged. On 11 April, they were transferred to Raffelding, never to fly again. The fighters stayed on the ground until 13 April due to a shortage of fuel. Then the 101/I and 101/II. FG went back into action, claiming five kills for the loss of two pilots.

On the morning of 16 April, the 101/I and 101/II FGs engaged ten La-7s and Yak-9s with neither side gaining any kills. The fourth formation started to take-off from Raffelding at 1405, when the Mustangs jumped them. One Bf 109K, shot down a P-51, while still retracting its wheels. The Mustangs; however, scored three kills in the air. Meanwhile, one of the Messerschmitts returning from a mission, was warned of the raid by radio. He tried to land at the western end of the airfield with a tail wind, but crashed and his Bf 109 was a total write-off. The P-51s went on to destroy several Bf 109Gs and about twenty Fw-190s on the ground. The anti-aircraft gunners reported shooting down seven Mustangs and damaging another two, using aircraft machine guns mounted on wooden posts along the airfield's perimeter. Among the damaged American aircraft was the Mustang flown by Lieutenant Colonel Joe Thury. The irony was that Thury was of Hungarian decent.

The Fighter Wing achieved its last victory on 17 April 1945, when 1st Lieutenant Kiss shot down a Yak-9. Hungarian fighters took-off for the last time on 22 April. Three of the eight aircraft turned back because of mechanical problems, followed by their wing men. The remaining three aircraft carried on and found a number of Soviet fighters. In the battle that followed, one was hit and made a belly landing, the other two were declared missing in action.

On 23 April, a number of new fighters were received; however, six of them were burned after an American low-level attack on the airfield. The remaining aircraft were set on fire by the Pumas, before they marched into captivity on 3 May. The men of the 102. F-FG followed them into the POW camp on 5 May 1945.

Aircraft Of The RHAF

Fighters

From 1936 on, Hungary made several purchases of Fiat CR 32 fighters from Italy to bring its planned fighter units up to strength. Each squadron within the fighter wing was to consist of three, three plane flights (nine fighters). It was planned that the number of aircraft in each squadron would be increased to fifteen plus three spares at a later date.

On 14 June 1936, ten Italian CR 32 formations demonstrated acrobatic flying at Mátsásföld, to prove the CR 32s excellent flying characteristics. The Hungarian order was delivered, bearing civil registrations, beginning in the Spring of 1936. Seventy-six were delivered in 1936, followed by another eight in 1938. After the Austrian *Anschuss,* thirty-six ex-Austrian Air Force aircraft were delivered to the RHAF. There were relatively few accidents with the type and, like any other biplane, it had good turning qualities and was well liked by the pilots. The CR 32 was armed with a pair of machine guns and the RHAF experimented with arming the aircraft with twelve 2 kg 33.H. anti-personnel bombs to give it a fighter-bomber capability. By the beginning of the Second World War, the type was almost outdated and their participation in the fighting was very limited. Surviving aircraft were turned over to fighter training schools for use as advanced trainers.

The 1 Fighter Wing was organized as follows:

Wing Commander: Colonel István Modory

1/1 Fighter Group Commander: Major János Schwáger. Home Base: Börgönd Field
    1/1 Fighter Squadron Commander: 1st Lieutenant Lajos Batáry
    1/2 Fighter Squadron Commander: 1st Lieutenant Istvan Timar
    1/3 Fighter Squadron Commander: 1st Lieutenant Mihály Nagy

1/II Fighter Group, Home Base: Kecskemét Airfield
    1/4 Fighter Squadron Commander: 1st Lieutenant Pál Batáry
    1/5 Fighter Squadron Commander: 1st Lieutenant Mátyás Szabò
    1/6 Fighter Squadron Commander: 1st Lieutenant Elek Ivàtskovits

The tense political situation in Europe during 1939 and the outdated nature of the CR 32 led the RHAF to order eighteen Fait CR 42s through the Hungarian Military Attaché in Rome. These aircraft were purchased without any demonstration or testing. The CR 42 was one of the best fighters in Europe at the time and the first three were delivered on 17 June 1939. While flight trials were going on with these, a further fifteen were delivered; however, the Italians were unable to supply a two seat

The pilot of this camouflaged Fiat CR 32 is warming up the Fiat A30 liquid-cooled in line engine prior to take-off on another mission. The aircraft carries Black code numbers with Yellow shading and the squadron insignia on the fuselage. (Kovács)

trainer version. Engine problems led the RHAF to consider replacing the engine with the license-built Gnome-Rhone K-14 radial engine. Plans were also made to replace the armament with Hungarian-built, motor-driven machine guns. By the time the engine modifications were completed, the CR 42 had became outdated, since monoplane fighters were coming into service throughout Europe. Italy delivered sixty-eight CR 42s by 1940. A further two were acquired in 1942 in an exchange for a Yugoslavian S.M. 79 bomber that made a force landing in Hungary. A number of CR 42s took an active part in the early fighting in the Soviet Union.

Later, a number of CR 42s were pulled out of front line service and used as advance trainers. Plans were also made to use a number of CR 42s as night fighters, but they proved to be unsuitable for the task, even after they were equipped with radios.

In early 1944, the 102 Ground Attack Squadron was formed utilizing the surviving CR 42s. Bomb racks were installed under the wings and, although flight trials were carried out, the squadron never saw action.

The Germans released the Heinkel He 112 for export during 1939. Among the countries that were considered to be potential buyers was Hungary. The Heinkel demonstration aircraft performed at the Air Force Experimental Institute's airfield at Csepel (on the outskirts of Budapest) on 14 February 1939. During the demonstration, the aircraft crashed; however, a second aircraft was sent by Heinkel, which performed a very successful demonstration. As a result, sixteen He 112s were ordered for the RHAF. The first three aircraft were equipped with bomb racks after delivery. It was also recommended that the 20MM Oerlikon cannons be replaced with the rapid-firing Hungarian-built Danuvla 39MM cannons. Plans were also made to replace the aircraft's machine guns. The RHAF made an attempt to acquire the rights to license-build the aircraft, but, the Germans would not sell the rights. The rest of the He 112 order was canceled when Hungary decided to

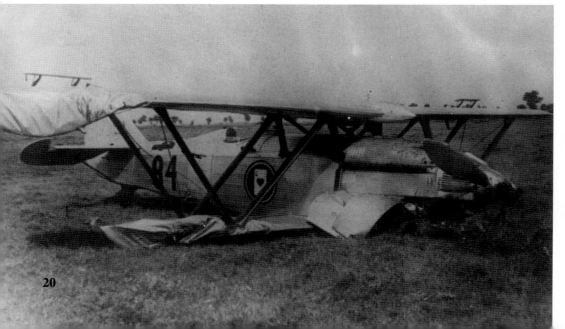

This Fiat CR 32 crashed landed ripping off the landing gear and badly damaging the nose and wing. The overall Silver aircraft carried a Black code number and the insignia of the 1/3 *Kör Ász* (Ace of Hearts) squadron on the fuselage. At this point the aircraft did not have Hungarian national markings applied to the fin. The aircraft number (84) and its overall Silver colo identify it as one of the thirty-six ex-Austrian Air Force aircraft delivered to Hungary after Austria was absorbed by Germany. (Kovács)

These Fiat CR 32s of the Kör Ász squadron carry the aircraft code on the fuselage in Black with Yellow shading. The CR 32 was armed with a pair of machine guns firing through the propeller arc and some were outfitted with twelve 2 kg 33.H. anti-personnel bombs to give it a fighter-bomber capability. By the beginning of the Second World War, the type was almost outdated and their participation in the fighting was very limited. (Punka)

purchase Raggiane Re 2000s from Italy. The only first line service that the He-112s saw was on 21 August 1940 when they were assigned to protect the rail lines in eastern-Hungary.

The Air Force High Command realized in 1939 that a the number of fighters that were ordered from Italy during 1938 would not fulfill their needs since their delivery was constantly delayed, making the aircraft obsolete before they were even delivered. Based on this, the Defense Council decided to purchase seventy Reggiane Re 2000 Falco fighters.

One of the reasons for this decision was that the Hungarians felt that they could not count on obtaining aircraft from Germany. Delivery of the Re 2000s began during the Spring of 1940 and, by the end of 1941, fifty-seven aircraft were on strength. The remaining thirteen were delivered in 1942. After going through various technical modifications, the Defense Ministry sent several aircraft, now named *Hèja* (Hawk), to the Soviet front for testing under combat conditions. These aircraft remained at the front until October of 1941. Almost a year later, the newly formed 2/1 Fighter Squadron went to the Soviet front equipped with eleven *Hèjas*. They were followed by the 1/1 Fighter Squadron in August of 1942. The Re 2000 stayed in front line service until the beginning of 1943, after that date, they were used as trainers.

In early 1940, a Hungarian delegation of technicians traveled to Italy to discuss the possibility of license-production of the Raggiane Re 2000. An agreement was reached and, after various modifications, production of the first twenty-five Mávag *Hèjas* got under way in late November of 1941. The first production aircraft made its maiden flight during October of 1942. The Hungarian-built aircraft were powered by the K-14 engine and had additional armor. By the end of 1944, 179-180 aircraft had been produced.

Hungarian-built *Hèja*s saw combat only once, when a few enthusiastic, but inexperienced pilots, attacked an American bomber formation on 13 April 1944. Even though the armament and the engine of the Mávag-built aircraft were better than the Re 2000, its performance was outdated by 1944 and the Hungarian formation was the losers in the engagement. After this, the Re 2000s were used solely for training.

A Hungarian Defense Ministry delegation began negotiations with Germany during 1941, to obtain license production rights for the Messerschmitt Bf 109. According to the plan, the fuselage of the Bf 109 would be produced at the Mávag plant. Half of the production would go to the RHAF, the other half to the Luftwaffe. Full production was planned to start twenty-two months after the signing of the agreement. The first production order was for fifty aircraft per month; however, because the necessary tools, machines and special materials were not supplied in time, production did start on schedule. The Defense

Ministry ordered thirty aircraft from Germany, but only three Bf 109Ds were delivered. The first Hungarian-built Bf 109G-2 was flown during 1942.

In the Fall of 1942, several Hungarian pilots received conversion training on Bf 109s on the Russian front. These pilots, under the command of lst Lieutenant Bánlaky, served as part of an experimental fighter squadron within the framework of JG 52. They saw action against advancing Russian troops from the beginning of 1943 on, with the Hungarian Bf 109F-4s being used as fighter-bombers.

During this period, 5/1 Fighter Group deployed 5/1 and 5/2 Fighter Squadrons to the front with Bf 109G-2. The personnel assigned to the Bf 109Gs came from other fighter units that had previously flown Re 2000s. The Group, commanded by Aladar Heppes, flew 1,560 sorties by the end of October, 1943, and scored sixty-seven kills in air-to-air combat. By the end of the year, the weather conditions became unfavorable and the crews were either replaced or sent home for a rest.

The fuselage and the landing-gear were Hungarian-built at the Hungarian Rail Coach Factory at Györ. The propellers, instruments, radios, armament were supplied by the Germans, as were the engines of early production aircraft. By the end of 1943, the engines were being produced in Hungary and only the canopies and instruments were brought in from Germany. During 1943, production switched from the Bf 109G-2s to the Bf 109G-6 and in 1944, to the Bf 109G-10 and Bf 109G-14, each equipped with a 30MM cannon. Eighty aircraft were pro-

This camouflaged Fiat CR 32 was assigned to the Fighter School at Veszprém airfield but still carried the markings of the Puma squadron on the fuselage. The aircraft carries late style national markings and codes that came into used during 1942. (Punka)

This Fiat CR 42 was camouflaged in Gray/Green/Brown on the uppersurfaces and had a very unusual segmented cowling. The aircraft was assigned to the *Kör Ász* (Ace of Hearts) fighter squadron based at Mátyásföld during the Summer of 1942 and carried the unit insignia on the fuselage below the cockpit. (Winkler)

This CR 42 of the Ace of Hearts Squadron, based at Kassa during 1941, had its fuselage code, V-204, applied German style lettering. The camouflage finish was also in the German splinter style and the squadron insignia was applied directly to the fuselage side without the usual White surround. (Winkler)

Captain László Tomor, commanding officer of the 2/4 *Kör Ász* (Ace of Hearts) Fighter Squadron boards his CR 42, coded V-206. The aircraft carries a Yellow fuselage identification band, required for Axis aircraft on the Russian front, behind the cockpit. The small Red stars were patches where his CR 42 was hit by Russian anti-aircraft fire on an earlier mission. (Petrick)

duced during 1943.

An American bombing raid on 13 April 1944 caused heavy damage to the factory. Prior to that date production had reached some 367 aircraft. After the bombing, with the exception of the final assembly line, the factory was dismantled and dispersed throughout thirty-four small villages. In July, the factory was bombed again, although an additional twenty to thirty aircraft were assembled from the parts on-hand before the factory was shut down. The shops were relocated in abandoned under-ground rock quarries in Budapest. By the Fall of 1944, production had reached one aircraft per day. When the Russian troops occupied the city at the end of the year, the total production of Hungarian-built Bf 109s had reached some 800 aircraft. Discussions had been held regarding license production of the Me 209, but this never progressed beyond the planning stage.

During April of 1944, the American bombers began flying over Hungary more and more often. The Allied formations flew over unintercepted until the German occupation of Hungary on 19 March 1944. During this same time period, two Hungarian fighter squadrons were re-equipped with Hungarian-built Bf 109Gs. The 1/1 Fighter Squadron at Szolnok took delivery of their aircraft on 23 February 1944. The 2/1

A number of Fiat CR 42s took an active part in the early fighting in the Soviet Union The Yellow tail and Yellow cowling of this CR 42 were overpainted with Gray to tone down the aircraft for operations over Russia during the Summer of 1941. The Red fuselage codes were also oversprayed with a Green color. It also appears that the unit marking on the fuselage has also been partially overpainted to tone down its White background. (Punka)

A Fiat CR 42 of 1/4 Szent György (Saint George) Fighter Squadron with a Yellow fuselage band and Red fuselage code. When it first entered service, the CR 42 was one of the best fighters in Europe; however, by the time it went into combat with the RHAF over Russia the aircraft was outclassed by the Soviet I 16 fighters it encountered. The CR 42s were used mainly in the ground support role. (Punka)

Fighter Squadron, tasked with defending Budapest, received their Bf 109Gs somewhat earlier. Hungarian fighter pilots flew Hungarian-built Bf 109s during 1944, but by the end of 1944, because production stoppages due to the bombing, replacement aircraft were now supplied by the Germans from other factories. The two Hungarian squadrons fighting on the Russian front received their replacement aircraft directly from the Germans.

Most of these were used Bf 109Gs and by early 1945, German stocks were the only source of replacement aircraft. As Luftwaffe fighter wings were re-equipped with up-to-date aircraft and some of these new Bf 109Ks were also given to Hungarian squadrons.

Hungarian flown aircraft were, if the situation at the front permitted, repainted with the Hungarian White cross on a Black square and the Red/White/Green national colors on the tail. On many occasions; however, there was no time to apply these markings and the fighters flew with German markings.

Several Bf 110s arrived at Ferihegy Airfield (Budapest) for use in training Hungarian night fighter and fast bomber crews. These aircraft flew with German markings. Later, they received Bf 110G-2 trainers and the 5/1 Night Fighter Squadron was equipped with Bf 110G-4s which were flew with full Hungarian markings.

The 102 Fighter-Bomber Group (later Ground-Attack Group) received some seventy Focke Wulf Fw 190F-8 fighter-bombers between the end of 1944 and the Spring of 1945. Initially, all of these aircraft received

(Above & Below) This CR 42 nosed over on landing. It has the late style national insignia and Yellow Russian Front markings (rear fuselage band and wing tip undersides). The aircraft carried the fuselage code V.2 + 63 in Black. (Punka)

This CR 42 of 2/4 Tör (Dagger) Fighter Squadron suffered a broken starboard main landing gear leg on landing. The fuselage code, V-237, was in Red, oversprayed with Green. The aircraft was camouflaged with a Dark Green base oversprayed with a Light Green mottle. The unit marking was a White pennent with a winged dagger. (Punka

A Heinkel He 112B-1, fuselage code V.303, parked on a Hungarian airfield during 1940. The aircraft were delivered in overall Gray and camouflaged with Dark Green and Brown after arrival. A total of sixteen He 112s were ordered for the RHAF and the first three aircraft were equipped with bomb racks after delivery. The aircraft proved to be unsuitable and the only front line service that the He-112s saw was on 21 August 1940, when they were assigned to protect the rail lines in eastern-Hungary. (Kovács)

full Hungarian markings, including squadron badges. A number of aircraft received later flew with German markings. The last Fw 190s were blown up by their crews on the airfield at Raffelding, Austria.

Hungarian Fighter Codes

V.001, Messerschmitt Bf 109F/G (49)
V.060, Fiat CR 32 (ex-Austrian) (36)
V.101, Fiat CR 32 (76)
V.201, Fiat CR 42 (70)
V.301, Heinkel He 112 (4)
V.310, Messerschmitt Bf 109G (80)
V.401, Reggiane Re 2000 I (70)
V.471, Reggiane Re 2000 II (28)
V.502, Reggiane Re 2000 II (70)
V.601, Messerschmitt Bf 109D (3)
V.606, Reggiane Re 2000 II (81)
V.751, Messerschmitt Bf 109G-2 (48)
V.801, Messerschmitt Bf 109G-6 (98)
V.951, Messerschmitt Bf 110G-2 (3)
V.001, Messerschmitt Bf 109G-10 (99)
V.101, Messerschmitt Bf 109G-10/14 (99)
V.201, Messerschmitt Bf 109G-10 (21)
V.501, Focke Wulf Fw 190F-8 (70)

Night Fighters

M.102 Messerschmitt Bf 110G-4 (15)
Z.001* Messerschmitt Me 210Ca-l (12)
*were not numbered in numerical order

V 401 was the first Re 2000 Héja fighter aircraft delivered to Hungary by the Italians during early 1942. (Lasztóczy)

(Left) The Re 2000 Héja, fuselage code V-451, of the Experimental Fighter Squadron, was damaged in combat with German fighters over Russia during 1942. The Hungarian pilot. Lieutenant Pittenbacher was slightly wounded in the fight. The name Pitti was carried on the forward fuselage in White script. (Gyenes)

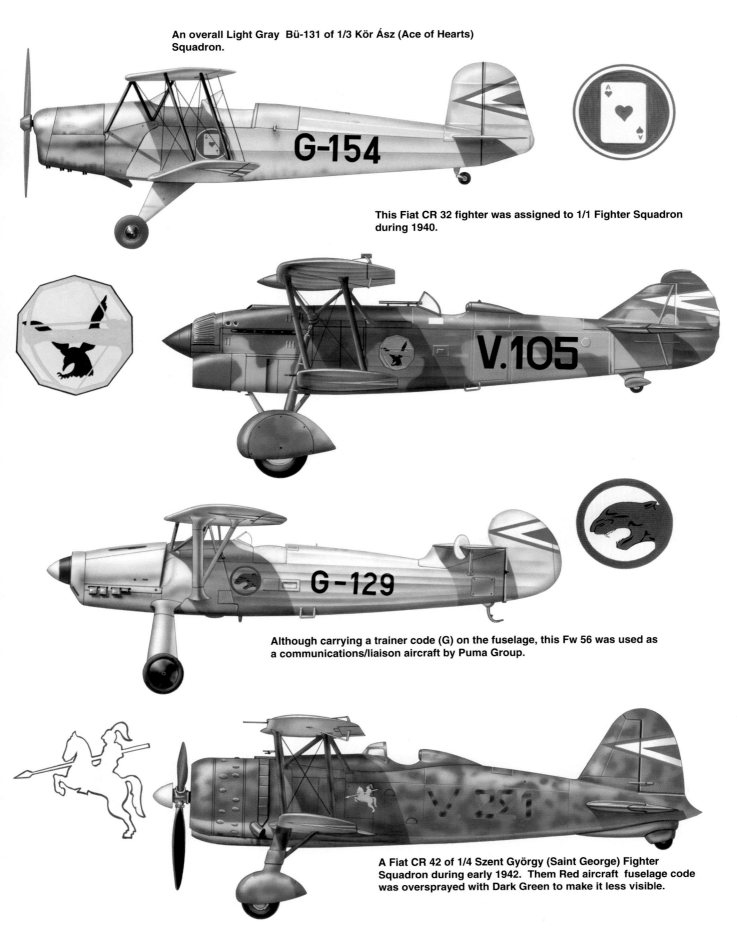

An overall Light Gray Bü-131 of 1/3 Kör Ász (Ace of Hearts) Squadron.

This Fiat CR 32 fighter was assigned to 1/1 Fighter Squadron during 1940.

G-154

V.105

G-129

Although carrying a trainer code (G) on the fuselage, this Fw 56 was used as a communications/liaison aircraft by Puma Group.

A Fiat CR 42 of 1/4 Szent György (Saint George) Fighter Squadron during early 1942. Them Red aircraft fuselage code was oversprayed with Dark Green to make it less visible.

25

These Re 2000s are being repainted, with their Yellow markings being removed and early markings being changed over. The aircraft were based at Poltava airfield in Russia. (Funár)

The Hungarians followed the German style of kill markings and the pilot of this Re 2000 is painting a victory stripe on the fin. The aircraft serial number was N.C. 273 and the fuselage code was probably V-407. (Gyenes)

This Re 2000 *Héja* made a wheels-up landing on Ilovszkoje airfield during February of 1943. The Black fuselage code was V.4 + 58 and the aircraft had no Yellow fuselage band. (Yerray)

(Left) A line-up of seven Re 2000 *Héja* fighters on a forward airfield somewhere in Russia during the early stages of the war. The first three aircraft in line all have names painted on the forward fuselage in White. (Kovács)

The first two digits in the fuselage code, V.4 + 40 . were Black while the second two digits were White. This Re 2000 *Héja* of 1.1 *Dongó* (Wasp) Fighter Squadron, 1/1 Fighter Group carries the unit marking on the fuselage and the Yellow fuselage band required for aircraft operating on the eastern Front. The aircraft was based at Ilovszkoje airfield during February of 1943. (Terray)

Salvage crews lift a damaged Re 2000 on to a flatbed rail car for transportation to the repair shops. This *Héja*. V.4 + 53 had the rudder, horizontal stabilizers and wings removed to make it easier to load. (Terray)

An old aircraft in new "clothes". This Re 2000, fuselage code V.4 + 05 was repainted at Szombathely with Dark Green uppersurfaces over Light Gray undersurfaces replacing the original Italian Sand and Green Mottle finish during 1943. (Punka)

This Re 2000 of 1/1 *Dongó* (Wasp) Fighter Squadron was a squadron or flight commanders aircraft, since it carried a radio mast behind the canopy. Not all aircraft were equipped with radios during 1942.

These men were students at Technical School, at Újvidék, during 1943. The Re 2000 was being used as an instructional airframe to train mechanics. The *Héja* carried the late style national markings and was painted overall Dark Green. (Punka)

A mechanic looks for a part from the fuselage of V.4 + 43 which was parked outside one of the Charkow airfield workshops for use as a source of spare parts to keep other *Héjas* flying. (Bagossy)

The Mávag-built Re 2000 *Héja II* was equipped with a WM 14 radial, engine, Gebauer machine guns and a modified cowling. This new production aircraft was based at Ferihegy during 1944. (Birkhoffer)

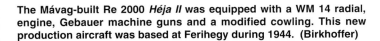

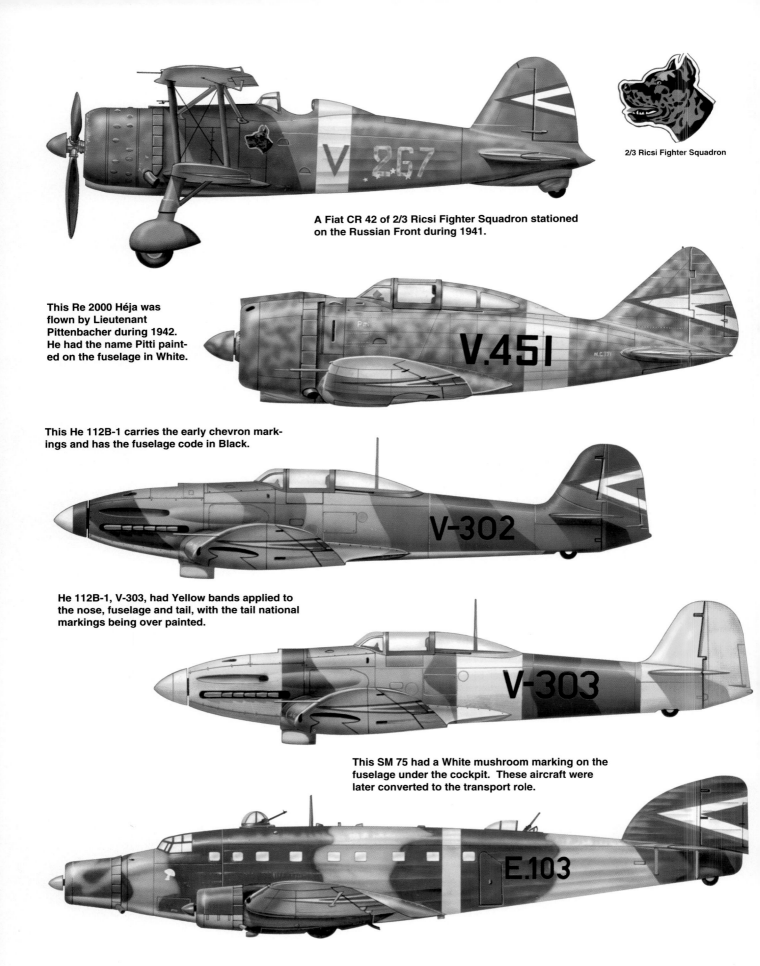

2/3 Ricsi Fighter Squadron

A Fiat CR 42 of 2/3 Ricsi Fighter Squadron stationed on the Russian Front during 1941.

This Re 2000 Héja was flown by Lieutenant Pittenbacher during 1942. He had the name Pitti painted on the fuselage in White.

This He 112B-1 carries the early chevron markings and has the fuselage code in Black.

He 112B-1, V-303, had Yellow bands applied to the nose, fuselage and tail, with the tail national markings being over painted.

This SM 75 had a White mushroom marking on the fuselage under the cockpit. These aircraft were later converted to the transport role.

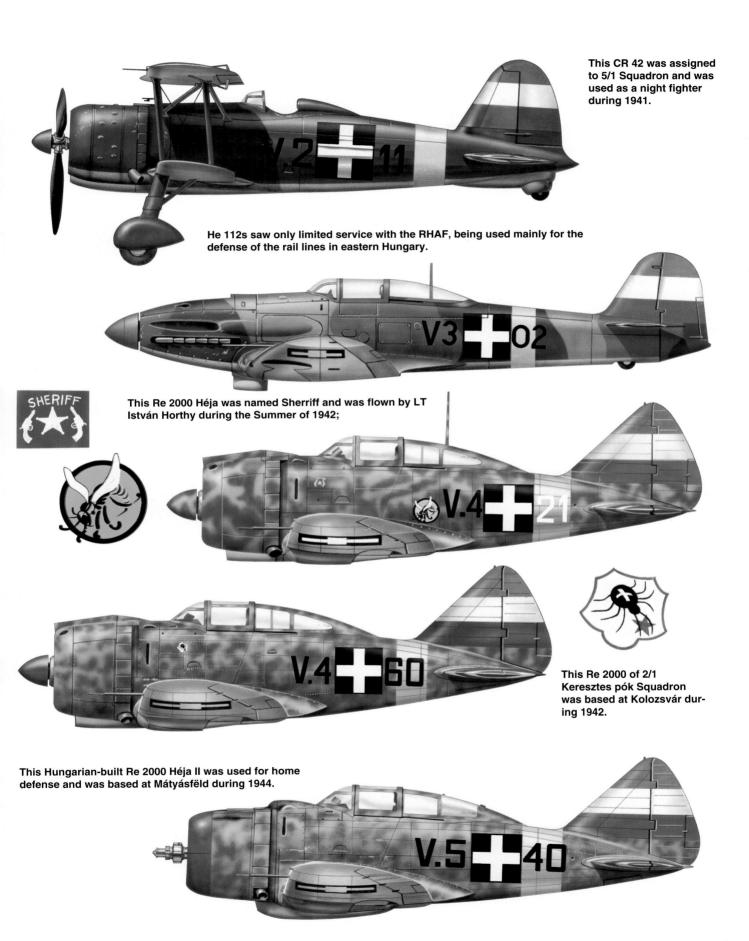

This CR 42 was assigned to 5/1 Squadron and was used as a night fighter during 1941.

He 112s saw only limited service with the RHAF, being used mainly for the defense of the rail lines in eastern Hungary.

This Re 2000 Héja was named Sherriff and was flown by LT István Horthy during the Summer of 1942;

This Re 2000 of 2/1 Keresztes pók Squadron was based at Kolozsvár during 1942.

This Hungarian-built Re 2000 Héja II was used for home defense and was based at Mátyásföld during 1944.

Corporal Faludi standing in the cockpit of his Hungarian-built Re 2000 *Héja II* during 1943. The bulges on the upper fuselage covered the gun breech for the Hungarian-built Gebauer machine guns. (Faludi)

This Re 2000 *Héja II* is equipped with a radio mast behind the sliding canopy section, indicating that it belongs to a squadron or flight commander. Most *Héja IIs* had the rearmost canopy section glass deleted.

The landing gear failed on this *Héja II* when it became mired in the mud on landing after a test flight from Ferihegy airfield during 1944. (Kovács)

A *Héja II* pilot prepares to start his engine prior to a test flight. The Hungarian-built variants of the Re 2000 saw little actual action, with their only recorded combat taking place on 13 April 1944 against American bombers (Punka)

A ground crewman assists Mávag test pilot, Takátsy, prepare for a flight from Budaör airfield with a new production *Héja II.* This aircraft was one of the second batch of seventy Re 2000s built under license in Hungary. (Takátsy)

This Messerschmitt Bf 109F-4B carries a temporary White Winter camouflaged and has the main landing gear doors removed. This was done because mud would collect between the door and the landing gear leg when operating from dirt fields in Russia during the Spring thaw. A overpainted "J" radio code letter is visible under the wing outboard of the wheel well. (Vásárhelyi)

Vitéz Dezsö Szentgyörgyi prepares to close the canopy of his winter camouflaged Bf 109F-4b on the Russian front during early 1943. (V. D. Szentgyörgyi Jr.)

This Messerschmitt Bf 109G-6, based at Kharkhow during 1944, was flown by Lieutenant László Molnár, who had the name of his girl friend Erzsike painted on the fuselage just behind the cockpit. (Vásárhelyi)

A pair of Messerschmitt Bf 109Gs on the ramp at the forward repair and maintenance station in the Soviet Union during 1944. The aircraft in the foreground is V.3 + 68, while the aircraft in the background up on jacks was V.3 + 72, which had suffered a landing gear failure. (Dr. Koos)

A ground crewman poses in front of a Bf 109G-6 that had oversized Hungarian national markings on the wing undersurfaces. This was probably done to make sure that friendly anti-aircraft gunners would be able to identify the fighter. (Dr. Koos)

This Caproni Ca 135bis bomber served with 3/5 Bomber Squadron on the Russian Front during the Summer of 1942. It carried the Witch unit marking on the nose in Black.

3/5 Bomber Squadron

This Fieseler Fi 156 Storch of 1 Courier Squadron served on the Russian Front during 1944.

A Ju 88A-4 bomber of 102/1 Bomber Squadron. The aircraft served on the Russian Front during the Summer of 1944.

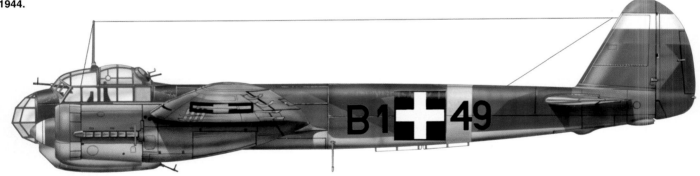

The Hungarian 1/1 Long Range Reconnaissance Squadron used this Ju 88D over the Russian Front during 1943.

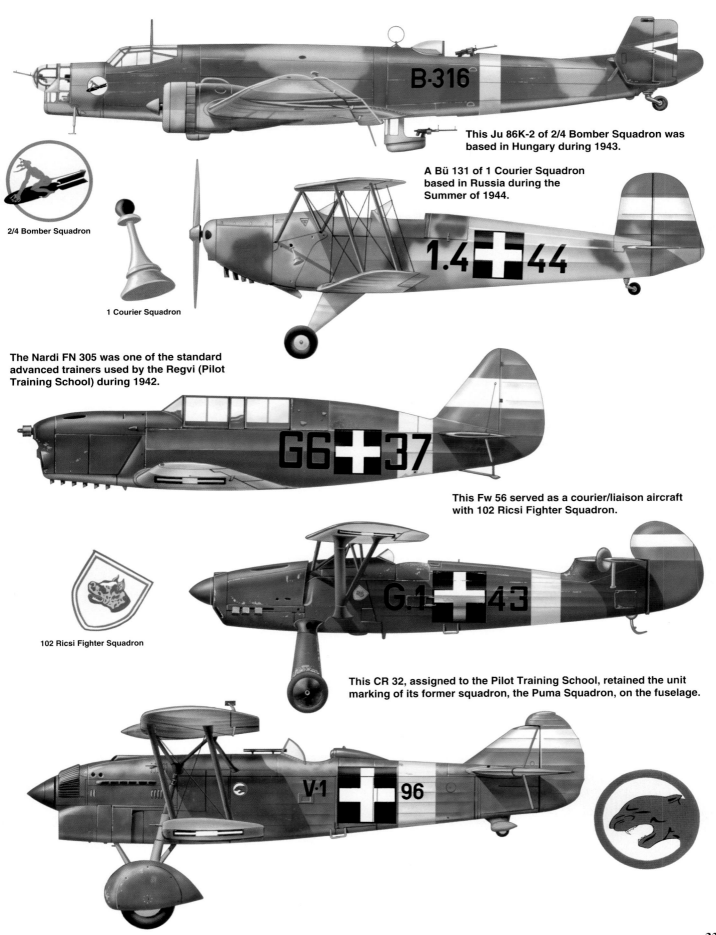

B-316

This Ju 86K-2 of 2/4 Bomber Squadron was based in Hungary during 1943.

2/4 Bomber Squadron

A Bü 131 of 1 Courier Squadron based in Russia during the Summer of 1944.

1 Courier Squadron

1.4✠44

The Nardi FN 305 was one of the standard advanced trainers used by the Regvi (Pilot Training School) during 1942.

G6✠37

This Fw 56 served as a courier/liaison aircraft with 102 Ricsi Fighter Squadron.

102 Ricsi Fighter Squadron

G.1✠43

This CR 32, assigned to the Pilot Training School, retained the unit marking of its former squadron, the Puma Squadron, on the fuselage.

V·1✠96

Red Seven was a Messerschmitt Bf 109G-6 station at Ferihegy for defense of the Hungarian capital, Budapest. (Punka)

This Bf 109G-6, based at Charkow, had a Black spinner with a White spiral design. (Dr. Koos)

Ground crewmen turn the inertia starter on a Bf 109G of 5/1 Puma Fighter Squadron. At this point in the war the squadron insignia was reduced in size. This was done because the Red and White insignia made a very good aiming point for enemy gunners. (Karátsonyi)

This Bf 109G suffered a landing accident at Budaörs airfield. The Messerschmitt in the background carries the fuselage code V.7 + 85. (Karátsonyi)

German and Hungarian Bf 110G-4 crew members pose in front of a Messerschmitt Bf 110 at Ohlau airfield during night fighter training in 1944. (Sárhiday)

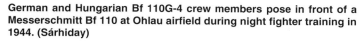

A Hungarian Bf 110G-4b night fighter crew pose with their camouflaged aircraft at Wiener Neustadt airfield during early 1945. The aircraft has a Black spinner with a White spiral design. (Hungarian Air Museum, Canada)

This Fw 190F-8 of 102/2 Fighter-Bomber Squadron has a White 20 on the nose. The aircraft was flown by Lance-sergeant Timler during January of 1945. The aircraft carries a bomb on the underfuselage bomb racks. (Stahl)

Lance-sergeant Tizekker of the 102/2 Fighter-Bomber squadron climbs out of his Focke Wulf Fw 190F-8 (fuselage code White 65) named Pöttöm (Tiny). The name was carried in White script on the nose gun cowling. (Banai via Punka)

Bombers

A Hungarian military delegation traveled to Germany in 1935 to discuss the availability of modern aircraft types that would be available for purchase. The Heinkel factory's offer to produce the aircraft for Hungary powered by Hungarian-built K-14 engines, only partially satisfied the delegation for two reasons. First, they would still have to purchase the license for the contra-rotating engines on the Heinkel 111 bomber and secondly, although the Heinkel He 51 fighter showed a speed increase when powered by the K-14 engine, it still demonstrated a poor turning capability.

The Germans were hinting at larger supply of military hardware if an agreement was reached and the Hungarians felt that it would be wise to consider a purchase of Ju 86 bombers, the next aircraft on their shopping list. The plan was to equip seven bomber squadrons with the Ju 86, with no reserves and, as a result, sixty-three aircraft were ordered in 1936.

The Junkers factory agreed to power the aircraft with K-14 engines and aircraft deliveries were delayed because the engines were not supplied on time. The last of the Ju 86K-2s were delivered on 30 June 1938. The aircraft's defensive armament, Gebaur machine guns, were installed in Hungary after delivery. The aircraft were delivered in civil registrations and did not enter military service until April of 1938. Crew training continued in spite of the many mechanical problems encountered with the aircraft.

The Ju 86s saw action in March of 1939, when Hungary regained some of her detached territories from the former Czechoslovakia. There were many border incidents between the newly formed state of Slovakia and Hungary. On 20 March 1939, Slovakian aircraft attacked Hungarian troops and the Hungarian Air Command decided to retaliate by attacking Slovakian airfields. On the afternoon of 24 March, the aircraft of the 3/II Light Bomber Group's 3/4 and 3/6 Bomber Squadrons and aircraft of the 2/II Light-Bomber Group took-off on a mission escorted by fighters of 1/1 and 1/2 Fighter Squadrons. Fourteen bombers attacked their targets and a number of Slovakian aircraft were set on fire.

Combat actions prior to 1941 were demonstrative in character. Real force was shown on 12 April 1941, when twelve aircraft of the 4/4 Bomber Squadron carried out attacks against the fortified Yugoslavian front lines.

On 27 June, a unit consisting of three Caproni Ca 135s and two Ju 86s attacked the Stanislav (Soviet Union) airfield (with poor results). The second attack, directed against Striy by sixteen bombers of the 4/II Bomber Group on 29 June, was successful. On twenty-seven occasions the Ju 86s saw action, flying more than one hundred sorties. Of these, ninety-seven were actual bombing missions. The Ju 86s were taken out from front line service during 1942 and the bomber units were reorganized. The Ju 86s were modified for transport, training and reconnaissance duties, or were used as liaison aircraft. The last of the Ju-86s were destroyed by American raids on the ground.

The RHAF ordered thirty-six Caproni Ca 310 light-bombers during 1938. Three of these aircraft were used in mock war trials at Szombathely in September of 1938. The brand new aircraft were plagued with many problems and proved to be unreliable. As a result, they were returned to Italy. The Caproni factory made a new offer and agreed to deliver thirty-six Caproni Ca 135bis aircraft, crediting

A Junkers Ju 86K of 2/3 *Repülö Buzogány* (Flying War Hammer) Bomber squadron. The aircraft carried a three tone camouflage scheme of Sand Brown/Gray/Dark Green uppersurfaces over Light Gray undersurfaces. (Punka)

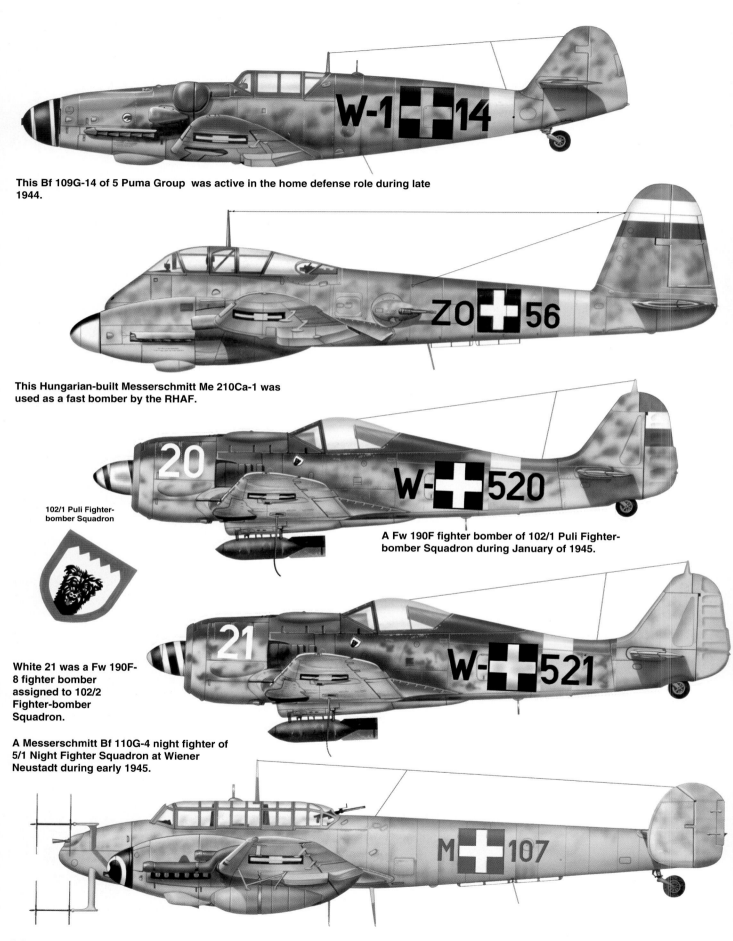

This Bf 109G-14 of 5 Puma Group was active in the home defense role during late 1944.

This Hungarian-built Messerschmitt Me 210Ca-1 was used as a fast bomber by the RHAF.

102/1 Puli Fighter-bomber Squadron

A Fw 190F fighter bomber of 102/1 Puli Fighter-bomber Squadron during January of 1945.

White 21 was a Fw 190F-8 fighter bomber assigned to 102/2 Fighter-bomber Squadron.

A Messerschmitt Bf 110G-4 night fighter of 5/1 Night Fighter Squadron at Wiener Neustadt during early 1945.

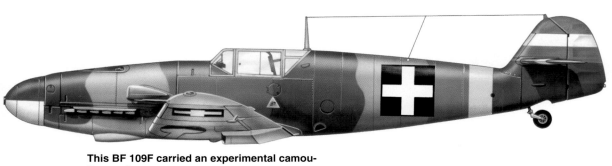

This BF 109F carried an experimental camouflage scheme.

This Bf 109F-4 was flown by György Debrödy on the Eastern Front. Debrödy was an ace with twenty-six kills.

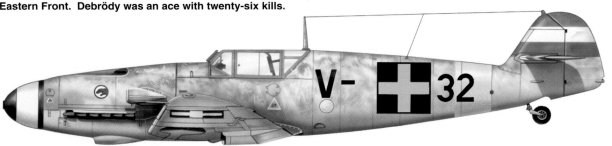

This Bf 109F-4 fighter-bomber of 5/1 Puma Squadron carried a small unit marking on the nose during February of 1943.

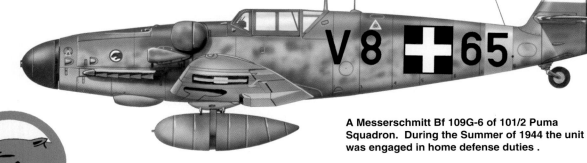

A Messerschmitt Bf 109G-6 of 101/2 Puma Squadron. During the Summer of 1944 the unit was engaged in home defense duties .

101 Puma Fighter Group

Black 66, a Bf 109G-6 flown by LT László Molnár, carried the name Erzsike in Black just behind the cockpit. Molnár was an ace with twenty-three kills.

A Junkers Ju 86K of 3/3 Sárkány (Dragon) Bomber Squadron parked on the grass at Budaörs airfield. (Szij)

Hungary for the returned Ca 310s. In 1940, the aircraft were delivered. Ten of these had been manufactured in 1939, but the rest were new production aircraft, right off the assembly lines. The aircraft's Regia Aeronautica registrations were MM 21565 to MM 21596 and the last four were MM 21946 to MM 21949. The first squadrons were re-equipped with the Ca 135s during 1940. It soon became apparent that the factory had not thoroughly checked the aircraft before delivery. There were numerous problems with the Piaggio engines, while the bomb racks and the bomb aiming devices were delivered late. About half of each bomber squadrons strength was under repair most of the time. Because of the constant problems with the aircraft, only one squadron was left operational by 1941 and the air force placed a new order with the Italian factory. This second batch of thirty-two aircraft arrived during 1942, with the Italian registrations MM 21950 to MM 21981. The Ca-135s were in action constantly from 1941 until September of 1942. From that time on they were used as advanced trainers, although some of them remained in front line service. The last military action by the Ca 135 came when three aircraft launched a mission against Soviet partisans (guerrillas) on 2 August 1943. After they returned to Hungary, the aircraft were dispersed on the airfield at Nadudvar, near Debrecen. Here, it was hoped that they would not be subject to bombing attacks. About twenty of them; however, were destroyed by an American surprise fighter attack on 15 September.

The Fall of 1942 brought a number of changes to the Hungarian

A group of young officers pose on the wing of a Ju 86K used for bomber pilot training. This aircraft is unusual in that the propeller blades are unpainted natural metal (Lászay)

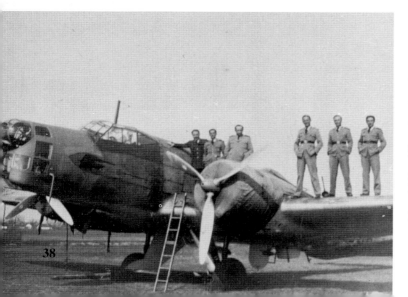

bomber forces. There were enough Ca 135s on hand to equip the two independent bomber groups, each consisting of four squadrons, but by this time they were so outdated that using them against the increasingly stronger Soviet anti-aircraft and fighter defenses would have been sneer suicide. The Germans were not pressuring the Hungarians to use their outdated Capronies in the front lines and promised to supply the front line Hungarian flying forces, including the bomber units, with more modern German aircraft. The stipulation was that the aircraft, although fully paid for by Hungary, could not be used anywhere else but on the Eastern Front.

Personnel of 4/l and 3/l Bomber Squadrons were given conversion training on the Junkers Ju 88A by IV/KG 3 in Istres, France, beginning in late 1943. After completing the conversion course, 3/l Bomber Squadron was transferred back to the Russian front. The Ju 88A-4s remained in service until mid-1944. The Germans also supplied a number of Ju 88C-6 fighters. After mid-1944, the aircraft were withdrawn from the front lines. A Luftflotte 4 report indicated that fifty-one Ju 88s had been delivered to the Hungarians by March of 1944.

The success of the German "Blitz" in September of 1939 impressed Hungarian military officials. Although the Hungarian government sym-

A three tone camouflaged Junkers Ju 86K on the ramp at Szombathely airfield. The aircraft carries a Yellow Eastern Front fuselage band theater marking and has the Yellow fuselage code, B.352, overpainted with Green. Ju 86s did see limited action on the Eastern Front during the early stages of the war, but were taken out from front line service during 1942 when the bomber units were reorganized. A number of Ju 86s were modified for transport, training and reconnaissance duties. (Punka)

pathized with the Poles and did what they could (almost 1,000 Polish flying personnel escaped through Hungary to the Allies), they could not ignore the fact that one of the most effective weapons spearheading the victory in Poland was the Junkers Ju 87 Stuka dive-bomber.

In 1940, four Ju 87Bs were ordered from Germany, followed by a second order for another twenty aircraft which was placed within the framework of a military financial credit plan. The Germans accepted the order, but did not give a delivery schedule. In the event, only two Ju 87Bs were delivered during the Summer of 1940. After testing by the Air Force Experimental institute, the aircraft were transferred to the 3/1. Bomber Group. Basic training was conducted on CR 32s and WM 21s before transitioning to the Ju 87. The two Ju 87Bs were only used for dive-bombing training. Meanwhile, a German-Hungarian Mutual Armament Program pushed the license-production of the Me 210 into the foreground and the Air Force gave up the idea of using the Ju-87s in front line service. The Germans handed over an additional four used Ju 87As for training purposes in early 1942.

In 1943, the Hungarian dive-bomber squadron was unexpectedly transferred to the front, where the Germans equipped the newly transferred squadron with Ju-87Ds. The 2/2 Dive-Bomber Squadron consisted of four three-aircraft flights. The unit arrived at Kiev by train during

May of 1943. Here they went through a month of tough training. Then they picked up their new aircraft, eleven Ju 87D-3s and a single Ju 87D-5, in Odessa. Their first action took place on 3 August against partisans hiding in the Bryansk forest

After this mission, the Hungarian squadron was transferred to II/StG 77, based in Poltava. The Hungarian dive-bomber squadron that was created by "necessity" achieved an unsurpassed record in the history of the RHAF. From the beginning of August until 22 October, they flew 1,200 sorties and dropped 800 tons of bombs. They lost six-and-a-half crews and fifteen out of the twenty-one Ju 87 D-3s and D-5s. In the air, they shot down two Lavochkin La-5s and one P-39 Airacobra. The squadron was recalled to Hungary during early January of 1944. The new 102/2 Dive-Bomber Squadron started its training in April on the remaining Ju 87s and on several newly arrived Ju 87B-ls. In May, the squadron received an additional twelve Ju 87D-5s. They were ordered to the front on 16 June and made their first combat sortie, for 1944, on 30 June. In the next two months, the 102/2 Squadron flew a total of forty-seven missions, dropped 150 tons of bombs and lost four aircraft. The squadron stayed at the front until the end of August when they turned over their remaining Stukas to 102/l Squadron in Krakow, Poland. After retraining on the Ju-87s, 102/l Squadron was returned to

This Caproni Ca 135 made a forced landing not too far from a village with engine failure. The aircraft, coded B530, of 3/5 Bomber Squadron, had the old chevron national insignia overpainted on the fin. (Kovács)

Armament crews of 4 Boszorkány (Witch) Squadron prepare bombs for loading into the bomb bay of a Ca 135 on the Russian Front. (Sinka)

This Mávag-built Re 2000 (Serial 11-035) Héja II carries a Sand Brown with Dark Green mottle camouflage while operating in the home defense role during 1943 and early 1944. (Bencso)/

This Messerschmitt Bf 109F was painted in an experimental camouflage scheme of Gray/Dark Brown/Dark Green uppersurfaces. (Punka)

This Dark Green Arado Ar 96B carried a Yellow Eastern Front fuselage band indicating that it was probably used as a liasion aircraft rather than a full time trainer. (Bencso)

This Mávag Héja II runs up its engine at Ferihegy airfield during 1943. The aircraft carried oversized national insignia on the under-surfaces of the wings and Yellow wing tips. (Bencso)

A Messerschmitt Bf 109G-2 parked on the grass Ferihegy airfield. The aircraft in the background are Re 2000s camouflaged in overall Dark Green. (Bencso)

A Messerschmitt Me 210Ca-1 fast bomber parked on the grass on a Polish airfield during the Summer of 1944. Z0 + 65 has its bomb bay open. (Winkler)

A pair of Junkers Ju 86Ks of 3/5 Bomber Squadron on a forward air-field camouflaged with trees. The aircraft in the foreground was coded B-5 + 42 (Serial M.M. 21955). Kovács)

Hajduszoboszló, Hungary. A short time later they relocated to Börgönd where their Stukas were destroyed during an American low-level fighter attack on 12 October 1944. At the end of April, the Germans organized a Hungarian Alert Squadron, equipped with Ju-87G-ls; however, the squadron never saw action.

In June of 1941, the Germany and Hungary signed an agreement for the license-production of the Messerschmitt Me 210 in Hungary. The plan was to produce some 900 aircraft; one during 1942, fifty-seven during 1943 and during 1944 some 213 aircraft were produced. Of the total production, 160 were delivered to the RHAF. Production of the Me 210 was to switch to the Me 410 after 300 aircraft had been built; however, this plan did not materialize. The American bombing attacks at first slowed production, then finally stopped it. The factory produced both fast bomber and reconnaissance variants as well as a few heavy fighters (destroyers). The destroyer Me 210s were armed with a 40MM cannon and a three 152MM rocket launchers under each wing. Production of the Me 210 in Hungary continued until October of 1944.

In late 1943, the 5/l *Bagoly* (Owl) Experimental Night Fighter Squadron was formed at Ferihegy under the command of Captain Adám Krudy, with six to nine Me 210s (without radar equipment). The commander of the Air Force Experimental Institute, Lieutenant Colonel Lòrand Dòczy, organized a Me 210 destroyer squadron on 4 April 1944, with the aircraft being flown by institute test pilots. The destroyer and the night fighter squadrons suffered such heavy losses from American escort fighters on 13 April 1944, that they were not used in combat again.

In March of 1944, the 102/l *Sas* (Eagle) Fast Bomber Squadron was formed in Poland. It followed a short time later by 102/2 **Tigris** (Tiger) squadron. The fast bomber squadrons were expanded with formation of 102/3 *Villám* (Lightning) Squadron at the end of 1944. The three

This Ca 135 made a belly landing near Debrecen (Hungary), ripping off the nose glass, starboard landing gear and starboard propeller. (Lászay)

Mixed Hungarian and German markings are carried on this Ju 87D of the Hungarian dive-bomber squadron. The bombs in the foreground were made of cement for use in training. The aircraft's German radio code VQ + DO, was changed to B.7 + 05 once the aircraft received its full Hungarian markings. (Punka)

squadrons were then formed into 102 Fast Bomber Group, entering combat in early 1945. Their last aircraft were blown up at Pandorf, Austria when a shortage of fuel prevented their evacuation.

Bomber Codes

B. 101, Caproni Ca 101/3m (17)
B. 121, Junkers Ju 88A-4/C-6 (51)
B. 201, Budapest WM 16 (9)
B. 301, Junkers Ju 86K-2 (63)
B. 401, Caproni Ca 310 (36)
B. 405, Ju 88A-4 (later renumbered}
B. 501, Caproni Ca 135bis (68)
B. 601, Junkers Ju 87B-2 (2)
B. 603, Junkers Ju 87A-1 (4)
B. 607, Junkers Ju 87B-1 (12)
B. 631, Junkers Ju 87D-5 (1)
B. 632, Junkers Ju 87D-3 (13)
B. 645, Junkers Ju 87D-5 (2)
B. 701, Heinkel He 111 (2)
B. 701, Junkers Ju87D-5 (14)
B. 715, Junkers Ju 87D-3 (1)
ZB 01, Junkers Ju-87D-3/5 (15)
Z. 001, Messerschmitt Me 210Ca-1 (99)
Z. 101, Messerschmitt Me 210Ca-l (61)

Members of 102/2 Zuhanóbombázó század (Dive bomber squadron) pose along side a Junkers Ju 87D-5 (B.7 + 06) on an airfield in Poland. This aircraft was flown by Lance-sergeant Horváh and his gunner Lance-sergeant Hosszú. The pair flew some forty-four missions during their time with the squadron. (Stahl)

41

A mixed formation of a Junkers Ju 88A and Ju 88C heavy fighter over Poland during 1944. The Ju 88C is believed to have been coded B.1 + 47. (Bogáti)

This Ju 87D, coded B.7+07 (ex SN+ZA), was flown by Sergeant Penzes (middle) and his radio-gunner Lance-sergeant Tarlós in Poland during the Summer of 1944. This was the second aircraft for this crew, their first being shot down on 11 July 1944. The squadron insignia was a monkey setting on a hill with coconut tree. (Stahl)

Although it carried Luftwaffe markings and a German radio code (P. + EP), this Winter camouflaged Junkers Ju 88A bomber flew with a Hungarian crew. The Germans did not undertake common missions or fly in mixed units because the Hungarians did not speak German, making communications difficult. (Nagymarosi)

This Ju 88A carried unusual style numbers over its temporary Winter camouflaged scheme. The aircraft was used for dive-bombing attacks on the Eastern Front. The dark painted fuselage underside was also non-standard for Hungarian Ju 88s. (Kovács)

This late production Ju 88A-4 had its horizontal tail surfaces damaged by a Russian fighter over the Eastern Front. The underfuselage gunner's position was fitted with a 7.9MM MG 81Z twin gun and the aircraft is also fitted with EZ-6 direction finder antennas on the fuselage spine. (Punka)

A Hungarian Ju 88A-4 of 3/1 Bomber Squadron over the Russian Front during January of 1944. The aircraft carries no national insignia on the wing uppersurfaces and no Red/White/Green stripes on the horizontal tail surfaces. (Nagymarosi)

The Winter camouflaged Ju 88A-4 in the foreground has FuG 101 antennas on the underside of the port win. The Ju 88C heavy fighter in the background has oversized national insignia on the wing undersurfaces. Both aircraft were assigned to 3/1 Bomber Squadron. (Punka)

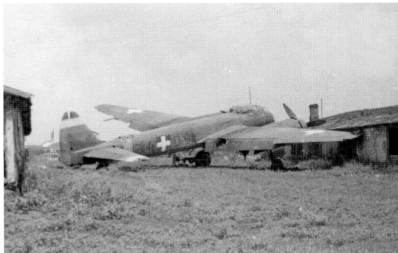

A pair of Junkers Ju 88C-6 heavy fighters of 3/1 Bomber Squadron in formation over the Russian Front during 1943. The propeller spinners of the aircraft in the foreground (B.1 + 22) were painted Red/White/Green. (Punka)

This heavily damaged Ju 88 bomber, coded B.4 + 09, has a large anti-aircraft shell hole in the starboard wing flap. On landing the aircraft rolled out without breaks and ended up between these barracks buildings. (Terray)

The first Hungarian Messerschmitt Me 210Ca-1 on Tököl airfield during the Winter of 1943-44. The Me 210Ca-1 was used mainly as a fast bomber, although a few saw service as night fighters and destroyers. (/Nagy Kornél)

This Messerschmitt Me 210Ca-1 (Z0 + 56) was assigned to either 102/1 *Sas* (Eagle) or 102/1 *Tigris* (Tiger) Fast Bomber Squadrons. It suffered a landing gear failure on landing. The aircraft carried standard Gray camouflage with full national insignia and striping. (Winker

43

This Me 210Ca-1 was destroyed on the ramp of the Messerschmitt works at Tököl airfield during 1944. This raid destroyed a number of parked aircraft and heavily damaged the factory. (Kiss)

The faired over nose gun ports on this Me 210Ca-1 at Hajdúböszörmény airfield during the Summer of 1944, indicates that it was probably used in the pilot training role. (Punka)

A Messerschmitt Me 210Ca-1 warms up its engines on Ferihegy airfield during 1944. (Franke)

A pair of two tone Gray camouflaged Me 210Ca-1s of 102/2 Tigris (Tiger) Fast Bomber Squadron parked in their snow covered revetments at Lesvár during the Winter of 1945. These aircraft have had their fuselage national insignia overpainted with Gray and they do not carry the national markings on the tail surfaces or Yellow Eastern Front markings. (Punka)

Long Range Reconnaissance Aircraft

The RHAF ordered eighteen Heinkel He 70 Long Range Reconnaissance aircraft during 1936. These were equipped with the Zeiss RMKS 7X7 inch (18x18cm) cameras and Telefunken 276F radios. The plan was to set up three long-range reconnaissance squadrons, consisting of six aircraft each. At the time, the He 70 was the fastest aircraft in its category. The Heinkel factory, at Hungarian request, re-engined each aircraft with a Hungarian-built WM K-l4 radial engine rather than the standard in-line engine. The first three aircraft arrived at Màtyàsföld in September of 1937. The Heinkels were deployed into two squadrons, the 1/1 Long-Range Reconnaissance Squadron (L-RRS) stationed at Budaörs and the 1/2 L-RRS posted at Kecskemet. The He 70s took part in the action against Yugoslavia and were also in use during the Russian campaign. Only one of the Heinkels was lost in combat, but other losses occurred due to accidents. The type was withdrawn from front line service at the beginning of the Russian campaign, but was used for training and as a target tug until the end of the war.

On 10 April 1941, a Yugoslav Dornier Do 17Ka got lost in thick cloud cover and made an emergency landing in Transylvania. After the Air Force Experimental Institute examined the aircraft, the RHAF put it into service assigning it the code J.101.

The long-range reconnaissance unit also used two Junkers Ju-86s. Their secret missions included the observation of the construction of fortifications, troop concentrations and airfield activities along the Hungarian border.

The two Ju 86s were transferred back to the bomber units after the arrival of the Heinkel He 111. The Air Force had requested twelve He-111s for use in the long-range reconnaissance role. Altogether, twenty

A Heinkel He 70 reconnaissance aircraft (coded F.4I0) of 1/2 Gólya (Storch) Long Range Reconnaissance Squadron in flight over Hungary. during the late 1930s. the unit was based at Kecskemet airfield. (Punka)

A He 70 of 1/1 *Hétmérföldes Csizma* (Seven League Boots) Long Range Reconnaissance Squadron on display at the international Fair in Budapest during 1942. (Kovács)

A pair of He 70 long range reconnaissance aircraft of 1/2 *Gólya* (Storch) Squadron, parked on the grass of their home base of Kecskemet air field. The aircraft are camouflaged in a three tone scheme of Dark Green/Gray/Brown uppersurfaces over Light Gray undersurfaces. (Punka)

He 111s were eventually ordered. Two of them arrived in July of 1940. Another four were delivered to the front in March of 1942, while a sixth was delivered at the end of 1942. The first two He 111Ps were intended to be used as bombers and were coded accordingly. But, because they were more in demand as reconnaissance aircraft, the Heinkels were returned and re-coded F.701 and F.702. They remained in service on the Russian front until early 1943 and participated in many missions. After an active service career, they were relegated to training duties. In 1944, the Air Force High Command planned to form a night attack group and equip its 2nd Squadron with He 111s. This so called Herder Group was stationed at Pápa, but saw no action. A Hungarian armistice delegation used one German marked Heinkel He 111 to slip into Italy during the Fall of 1944.

The Hungarian long-range reconnaissance units received ten used Dornier Do 215 aircraft from the Germans during 1943. These aircraft were used for only a short while and their crews were retrained to fly the Junkers Ju 88. From late 1943 on, the Dorniers were used for training purposes.

The 1st Independent Long-range Reconnaissance Group received their first Junkers Ju 88D-1 aircraft in November of 1942. These were former Luftwaffe aircraft and were flown with German markings for a period, because the cold weather and the pressing military situation did allow the crews the time to change the national markings. Later, a number of new Ju 88D-5s were delivered and near the end of the war, the Germans were ready to supply the long range units with a number of Ju 188s; however, this did not materialize before the war ended. From June of 1942 until the end of the war, the long-range reconnaissance squadrons

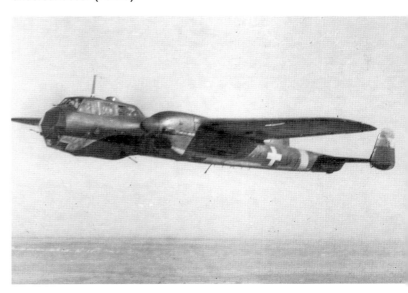

This Dornier Do 215 (coded F7 + 07) of 1/1 Long Range Reconnaissance Squadron was hit on a mission over Russia and streamed oil back over the vertical stabilizer. A short time later the port engine failed due to a lack of oil. (Molnár)

The crew of this Dornier Do 215B-1 is greeted by their ground crew after a reconnaissance mission over the Russian Front during the Summer of 1942. The aircraft was assigned to 1/1 *Hétmérföldes Csizma* (Seven League Boots) Long Range Reconnaissance Squadron. The RHAF operated three Do 215B-1 and seven Do 215B-4s in the reconnaissance role (Molnár)

A Do 215B-1 long-range reconnaissance aircraft delivered to 1/1 Seven League Boots Long Range Reconnaissance Squadron in Russia during 1942. These crewmen were radio-operator-gunners, two of them, Sergeants Molnár and Mészáros, were decorated with the Iron Cross, Second Class. (Molnár)

This long range reconnaissance Ju 86K, based at Marosvásáhely airfield in Transylvania, carried thirty mission markings on the tail in White. (Punka)

(Left) This Ju 88D reconnaissance aircraft nosed over on landing at a forward airfield in Russia during 1943. It still carried its former German markings, including the radio code SZ + OQ, which would be changed to F9 + 09, once the aircraft was repainted. (Benkó)

Ground crewmen prepare a Ju 88D for another reconnaissance mission over Russia. There are two cameras, a Rb 20/30 and a Rb 75/30 with their film cartridges, in the foreground. Although assigned to 1/1 Long Range Reconnaissance Squadron, the aircraft still carries its Luftwaffe markings. Quite often, the situation at the front did not allow time to repaint aircraft and they were operated in German markings or part Hungarian and part German markings for some time. (Benkó)

completed 1,000 to 1,100 missions and they scored twenty-three kills. On their last mission, with a German Ju 88, they photographed the devastated capital city of Hungary, Budapest. On 3 November 1944, the unit returned their aircraft to the Germans and disbanded.

According to an unofficial source, several Hungarian reconnaissance crews were trained by the Germans in Poland during the Summer of 1944 for special duties, such as dropping agents behind the front lines, using Ju 88s at night.

Long-Range Reconnaissance Aircraft Codes

J. 101, Dornier Do 17 Ka-3 (1)
F. 401, Heinkel He 70K (18)
F. 701, Heinkel He 111 P (6)
F. 707, Dornier Do 215B-1 (3)
F. 710, Heinkel He 111 P-6 (1)
F. 751, Dornier Do 215 B-4 (7)
F. 901, Junkers Ju 88D (23)

This group of Ju 88Ds of 1/1 Long Range Reconnaissance Squadron aircraft on an airfield in Russia display a mixture of markings, both German and Hungarian. The aircraft in the foreground, coded VG + DJ, would later become F9 + 08 when it received its full Hungarian markings. (Punka)

Ground crewmen prepare to refuel a Junkers Ju 88D-1 of 1/1 Long Range Reconnaissance Squadron on a forward airfield in Russia during 1943. This Ju 88D-1, coded F9 + 14, was unusual in that the fuselage code letters were outlined in White and the fuselage White cross was also larger than standard. The reason for these modifications is unknown. (Molnár)

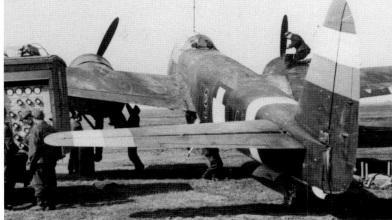

A Hungarian Junkers Ju 88D-5 Trop, coded F9+23, was formerly GM +CS (Werk Nr. 430059). The aircraft was damaged after being intercepted by Russian fighters on 5 October 1943. The observer, Lieutenant Visnyei, was killed, and the side panels in the cockpit were shot out. (Székely)

The 1/1 Long Range Reconnaissance Squadron flew its 500th mission over Russia on 2 July 1943. (Punka)

47

Short-Range Reconnaissance Aircraft

During 1936, Hungary had considered ordering nearly 200 aircraft from the Heinkel; however, the plan fell through when Hungary wanted to power the Heinkel He 51 fighter with the Hungarian-built K-14 radial engine. As it turned out, the narrow fuselage of the He 51 could not accommodate this engine and the contract fell through.

The other aircraft under consideration, was the single-engined He 46 short-range reconnaissance aircraft, which could take the K-14 engine. Thirty-six of these modified aircraft were purchased under the designation He 46E-2/Un. The engines were to be supplied by the Wiess Manfred factory in Budapest but, because the factory also supplied the engines for the Ju 86, the shipment to Heinkel was delayed. As a result of this delay, the first ten engines were obtained from the French Gnome-Rhone factory. French authorities would not permit the export of the engines to a German firm and the purchase had to be handled through a French agency, causing a number of problems before they were finally delivered to Hungary. In the end, only seven Gnome-Rhone powered aircraft were built. The first K-14 powered He 46 made its first flight during the Summer of 1937 and the first production batch was delivered to Hungary in December of that same year. Military trials, held in the early Summer of 1938, revealed that the aircraft was nose-heavy and a 154 pound (70 kg) sand bag had to be placed into the rear seat if an observer was not carried. Additionally, it was found that the operation of the rear machine gun required considerable strength and the effectiveness of the ailerons was poor. The relatively high power output of the K-14 engine could not be utilized to its full extent, because the 340 km/h top speed, guaranteed by the Germans, was restricted to 270 km/h. The fixed armament was replaced by a 26/31M Gebauer-

Men and aircraft of the 1/1 Long Range Reconnaissance Squadron prepare to move from Poltava to Kharkow during 1943. The Ju 88D-2 in the foreground still carries a German radio code (VE + AR) although it has full Hungarian national insignia. (Molnár)

Danuvia GKM twin-machine gun installation. The bomb bay equipment and radio were also added after delivery in Hungary. The first loss happened on 29 April 1938, when a civil registered (HA-HPO) He 46 burned following a forced landing.

As they were delivered, the aircraft were deployed to short-range reconnaissance squadrons and flew alongside Hungarian-built WM 21 *Sólyoms*. The Heinkels' unsatisfactory performance at the beginning was offset by their excellent combat performance in the Soviet Union. Considering the aircraft's outdated status, they were still successfully being operated during 1942. The aircraft, nicknamed *Ballagó* (Trudger), by Hungarian ground forces, carried out artillery observation, propaganda leaflet drops and even bombing, besides their normal photo-reconnaissance missions. The poorly armed and unarmored aircraft stood up against modern fighters and even achieved a few kills (3). In fact, the only He 46 lost in combat was brought down by anti-aircraft fire. After October of 1942, most Heinkels were transferred to training units. In 1943, the aircraft remaining in service with the 4th Short-Range Reconnaissance Squadron stationed at Ungvar, carried out several missions against the so called Kovpak (partisan units). A portion of the 4/2 S-RRS and other crews from various auxiliary units were sent to Germany during 1944 to form a new unit. This unit, called the 102 Night Ground Attack Squadron, was trained for nuisance flights with their remaining Heinkel He 46s and were in active service between 13 and 28 July, flying over Soviet territories. The last He 46s were blown up at the Wiener Neustadt airfield in March of 1945, just before the arrival of the Russian troops.

As a result of discussions between the Department of Air, the Wiess

Ground crewmen push a Heinkel He 45 biplane reconnaissance aircraft to a new parking spot. The aircraft carried a four tone camouflage finish and had a squadron insignia, a Red Devil on a White background, painted on the fuselage side below the cockpit. Even though it carries the insignia of II Lucifer Short Range Reconnaissance Squadron, the aircraft was assigned to the Reconnaissance School at this time. (Kovács)

Manfred Aeroplane and Engine Factory in Budapest and the Hungarian Rail Coach and Machinery Factory in Gyor, the production of the WM 21 reconnaissance-bomber, designed and improved in 1936-37, was begun at these factories. The Department of Air ordered thirty-six WM 21s during 1938, with production beginning during March-April 1939. The first aircraft made its maiden flight in December of that same year, although the Ministry of Defense had ordered an additional twenty-one aircraft before the maiden flight took place.

The mixed construction biplane was armed with two forward-firing, engine-driven Gebauer machine guns and a flexible ring-mounted machine gun in the rear cockpit. The bomb bay, equipped with a hand release mechanism, was located between the pilot's and gunner's seats and could carry anti-personnel and incendiary bombs. Four series of this type were built between 1939 and 1942. Thirty-nine aircraft, of the first three series, were powered by an 870-900 hp WM Gnome-Rhone engine, while the fourth series utilized a more powerful 950-1,000 hp radial engine. The production of the WM 21 ended in August of 1942, after a total production run of 128 aircraft. The WM 21 *Sólyom* reconnaissance aircraft served in independent and mixed reconnaissance squadrons and they suffered no losses due to enemy action. Beginning in 1942, a number of WM 21s were used in flying schools. A number of the remaining aircraft were deployed against the Kovpak partisan group during 1943. In the Spring of 1945, the surviving WM 21s were flown to Austrian airfields where they were destroyed.

This Heinkel He 45 reconnaissance biplane carries a Dark Green over Light Gray camouflage and Yellow Eastern Front markings. The aircraft, coded G.3+12, also carries the late 1942 style insignia, even through by this time most of the older He 45s had been transferred to training units inside Hungary. (Kovács)

The 3/1 S-RRS received their first Focke Wulf Fw 189 in 1943, and their service with the squadron was short lived. After only a few months in service, they were transferred to the 4/1 Squadron in the Spring of 1944. The twin-boomed aircraft had excellent flying characteristics and were flown by the Hungarian units until the Fall of 1944. Many of the aircraft retained their German markings, since the mutual German-Hungarian agreement provided for retention of German ownership of the aircraft.

At the end of 1944, the 4/1 S-RRS, later renamed as the 102 Reconnaissance Squadron, was retrained on Bf 109G-10/R2 photo-reconnaissance aircraft at Börgönd. Because of the approaching Russians, training was relocated to Kölleda airfield near Gotha, Germany. Here, the crews received ground instruction on the Me-262. A number of the retrained crews was deployed with a German-Hungarian unit in Quedlinburg and were flying reconnaissance missions over the American sector of the front. This mixed unit, men and aircraft, were captured by the Americans near Pocking, Austria, during May of 1945.

Short-Range Reconnaissance Aircraft Codes

F. 051, Focke Wulf Fw 189 (28)
F. 201, WM 21 Sólyom (99)
F. 301, Heinkel He 46 E/Un (36)
F. 601, WM 21 (29)
F. 801 (possible), Me 109 G-10 (12)

A line-up of Heinkel He 46E-2Un reconnaissance aircraft of the *Szárnyas bicska* (Winged Pocket Knife of Somogy) Short Range Reconnaissance Squadron parked on a forward airfield near the Carpatian mountains. The camouflage applied to these aircraft differed from aircraft to aircraft. (Kovács)

49

A line-up of newly delivered Heinkel He 46E-2Un reconnaissance aircraft of the I Close Reconnaissance Squadron. The aircraft were delivered from Germany in an overall Light Gray finish. The aircraft in the foreground, E.309, was lost on 10 February 1940. (Kovács)

(Left) The crew of a Heinkel He 46E-2Un pose alongside their aircraft in the Winter of 1940. The squadron insignia consists of a winged pocket knife with a camera suspended from it on a circular White field. (Kovács)

This He 46E-2Un carried a Yellow engine cowling and tail surfaces during the Yugoslavian campaign of 1940. The fuselage colors were Dark Green and Dark Brown with Green-Gray propeller blades. This aircraft was later damaged in a crash on 19 July 1941. (Kovács)

A pair of He 46s of I Squadron during the Winter 1940. The last digit of the fuselage code of the aircraft in the foreground was in Light Gray. (Kovács

A line-up of six He 46s of the II Lucifer Squadron during 1940. All the aircraft carried a three tone upper surface camouflage of Dark Green/Gray/Dark Brown with the squadron insignia carried on both sides of the forward fuselage. (Punka)

The gunner of the squadron commanders aircraft mans the rear cockpit machine gun of this He 46 of II Lucifer Squadron. The squadron marking was a angry Red Devil on a White background. (Kovács)

A pair of He 46s of *Holló* (Raven) Squadron on a grass field in Hungary during 1940. The He 46 in the foreground was coded F.307 and carried the squadron insignia under the rear cockpit. The camera bay in the fuselage underside was open. As was common during this period, both aircraft carry slightly different camouflage schemes. (Punka)

This He 46 encountered deep mud when it landed on Szombathely airfield and flipped over. The pilot and observer; however, were uninjured and walked away from the crash. The Yellow fuselage code code letters were overpainted with Green to tone them down and the squadron insignia was reduced in size. (Kovács)

He 46s of 102/1 Night Bomber Squadron fly formation on a training mission. This squadron was formed to do night harassment raids over Soviet lines. The aircraft were equipped with bomb racks under the fuselage for light bombs. (Szikszay)

This rear gunner of a Fw 189 is dressed in his "Summer uniform", shorts and a pistol and belt. The name on the side of the Fw 189, "Margit" was in White. (Czigány)

This was the first WM 21 Sólyom (coded P.6 + 91) of the second production series. The aircraft was used as a short range reconnaissance aircraft and was equipped with larger tires for operating from forward airfields. (Punka)

A Fw 189A-2 of 3/1 Táltos (Winged Horse) Short Range Reconnaissance Squadron on a forward airfield on the Eastern Front. The aircraft carried the fuselage code F.0 + 46. Fw 189s were not only used for reconnaissance, they also did light bombing missions against lightly defended targets. (Suttay)

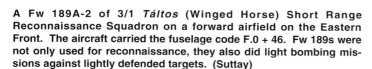

This Fw 189, coded F0 +64 was flown by Cornet Csapó (middle) and his crew over the Soviet Union during 1943. The bombs in the foreground could be carried by Fw 189s, but their primary mission was reconnaissance. (Csapó)

(Left) Low level reconnaissance missions over the Eastern Front in 1943 were very dangerous. This Fw 189 crewman points to the bullet holes in the rear canopy and fuselage made by a Soviet fighter. The large object above the rear gun barrel is a hooded gun sight. (Suttay)

1944.

The Arado Ar-96's introductory demonstration to the RHAF was performed by Arado factory test pilots in March of 1943, and led to Ministry of Defense order for the aircraft. By mid-1941, twenty-seven

A Romeo Ro 41 primary trainer undergoes maintenance work on the ramp at Szombathely airfield. The aircraft in the background are Focke Wulf Fw 56 trainers. The aircraft carries the chevron national insignia in six positions. (Takács)

Trainers And Liaison Aircraft

The standard trainer for the RHAF and the sport flying clubs was the small Bücker Bü 131 biplane, which was powered by an inverted four-cylinder in-line engine. During the Olympic Star Tournament, held in July of 1936, a number of these aircraft were flown in competition by Air Force officers, even though the aircraft themselves carried civilian registrations. After the war broke out, these aircraft were used for liaison work by the Hungarian Armed Forces, although they retained the I fuselage coding I = *Iskola* (school)]. The Bü 131 was license-built in Hungary and toward the end of the war, the last few aircraft remaining in service were flown to Austria by the staff of the Pilot Training School. Here they were grounded due to a lack of fuel. During 1939, a number of the radial-engined version of the Bücker were purchased by the RHAF, these aircraft received military coding.

From 1936 onward, the RHAF ordered the Focke Wulf Fw 56 high-wing monoplanes from Germany for use as the standard fighter lead-in trainer. The first eighteen aircraft were flown to Hungary by Hungarian crews carrying civilian registrations. Fighter squadrons received this new type in 1937. From 1939 on, these aircraft were given military codes with the letter G painted on the fuselage along with a number, (G = *Gyakorlò* or trainer). Later, they were also used for liaison duties. The Fw 56 remained in service until 1945.

The Italians offered the Nardi FN 305/315 during 1942, and the RHAF ordered fifty aircraft to replenish their diminished trainer inventory. The first aircraft arrived on 19 November 1942. An interesting little known fact was that the wood used in the production of the FN 305/315 was supplied to Italy by Hungary. By 1943, some fifty-two aircraft had been delivered and carried full Hungarian markings with the G trainer code being carried on the fuselage. The aircraft remained in service until

Although carrying trainer fuselage codes, these overall Light Gray aircraft are liaison aircraft assigned to 1/3 Kör Ász (Ace of Hearts) Squadron. The aircraft in the foreground is a Bücker Bü 131 trainer and the aircraft in the background is a Fw 56. The Bü 131 has a Natural Metal nose section. (Kovács)

Ar 96A-1s were delivered and an additional fifty-five were ordered from Arado at the end of 1941 (this later batch consisted of reconditioned ex-Luftwaffe aircraft). The first examples of the Arado Ar 96B-1 arrived during 1943, and the Defense Ministry placed an order for an additional 200 aircraft of this sub-type. Meanwhile, the *Mávag* (Hungarian Rail Coach Factory) was getting set-up to begin license manufacture the Ar 96B-1 and Ar 96B-3. By 8 August 1944, the factory had produced one Ar 96A and five Ar 96B-1s. Parts for the assembly of a further fifty aircraft were ready when an American bombing raid brought production to a halt. During the Spring of 1944, several Ar 96B-7s were delivered, which were used as liaison aircraft at various units until the end of the war. The Arado was used for both the advanced training role and liaison duties.

During 1936, the RHAF ordered six Bf 108 *Taifun* trainer/liaison aircraft. These were flown back to Hungary by the Hungarian crews later that same year. The aircraft were used for long-range communications duties, then later for liaison duties. One of the last Bf 108s of the 101/9 Fighter Squadron, carrying German code letters, escaped to Dübendorf, Switzerland, during 1945.

To help elementary bomber training, six Dornier Do 23s were delivered from Germany. Two of these were presented as gifts from the Germans. The Do 23s were used for short while, then they were turned over to the mechanics training school as ground instructional airframes. To avoid capture by the Russians, the last example of the Do 23 was flown by a mechanic back to northern-Hungary where it was later blown up.

In 1939, four Focke Wulf Fw 58 bomber-trainer and liaison aircraft were ordered from Germany, followed by an additional fifty aircraft in 1941. At the same time the RHAF began negotiations to produce the type under license. The first Hungarian-built Fw 58Ka-6 flew in September of 1942. About seventy Hungarian-built aircraft were completed before 1944 and these were used for basic training, instrument flying and liaison duties. During the war, the three Fw 58s that had been used by Hungarian Airlines, were taken over by the military and given military codes (S.001, S.002 and S.003) and assigned to 102/1 Transport Squadron.

In late 1944, a night ground attack group was formed and it was planned to equip one of the unit's squadrons with Fw 58s; however, the war ended before this plan could be put in action. On 27 February 1945, retired RHAF Major General Làszló Háry and his family escaped to Italy and surrendered to the Americans. His Blue Fw 58 carried the civil registration, HA-XBG. The type was used for training as late as the Spring of 1945, but on 10 April, most of the training machines were blown up, with only the liaison aircraft being kept in service.

Besides the previously named aircraft, the Air Force used many other types for training, and in some cases for liaison duties. One such aircraft was the *Levente*, a Hungarian built high wing trainer. Some seventy to eighty were manufactured and they were still in use during 1945. On 23 March 1945, a pilot of the 101/3 Fighter Squadron took off in a *Levente* from Veszprem airfield when Soviet Il-2s attacked him. In spite of serious wing damage, the pilot managed to elude his attackers and escape. Two other Hungarian pilots flew to Dübendorf, Switzerland from Linz, Austria in a *Levente* on 12 April 1945. The aircraft was used by the

Swiss Air Force after the war.

Another locally produced trainer was the **Honvéd I**, a twin-engined, four-seat liaison and radio-navigational trainer. Only two were completed and they were taken to Pápa, to avoid capture by the Russians, where they were later destroyed. The **Káplár** trainer was also intended to be a liaison and navigational trainer and five of these single-engined, high-winged, two-seat trainers were completed during 1941-42.

The standard liaison/observation aircraft of the RHAF, like many other Axis nations, was the Fieseler **Storch**. Hungary ordered fifteen during 1940 and another forty-three during 1941. The aircraft were all Fi 156Ca-3 series. During 1944, the ambulance version, the Fi 156Da-l, was also put into service. One of these, R 114, was the last plane to fly out from Ilovskoye airfield after it was encircled by Russian troops . Two aircraft of the 1st Independent Long Range Reconnaissance Group, R ll6 and R117, were both specially equipped for long range instrument flying with a 120 gallon auxiliary fuel tank.

Trainer/Liaison Aircraft Codes

Primary Trainers (*Iskola*)

I. 001, Bücker Bü 131D (60)
I. 101, Udet U 12 (10)
I. 111, WM 10/13 (9)
I. 121, Heinkel HD 22 (9)
I. 131, WM CVD (5)
I. 151, Bücker Bü 131A (5)
I. 161, Bücker Bü 131A (30)
I. 201, Bücker Bü 131B (70)
I. 281, RWD-8 (2)
I. 283, Praga E 39 (1)
I. 284, M 24 (2)
I. 301, *Káplár* (5)
I.351, *Levente I* (1)
I. 401, Bücker Bü 131D (100)
I. 501, Bücker Bü 131D (50
I. 551, *Levente II* (50)
I. 601, *Levente II* (30)
I. 701, Bücker Bü 181 (23)
I. 801, various sport aircraft (29)
I. 901, Caudron C600 (3)

Basic Trainers (*Kiképzö*)

K. 001, Brandenburg Cl (1)
K. 002, *Hungária* (12)
K. 101, Udet U 12B (18)
K. 201, Heinkel He 22 (12)
K. 301, WM C V. D/K (10)
K. 321, Focke Wulf Fw 58C (30)

Advanced Trainers (*Gyakorló*)

G. 101, Fiat CR30 and 30B (12)
G. 112, Focke Wulf Fw 56 (14)
G. 135, WM 20 (1)
G. 141, Focke Wulf Fw 56 (18)
G. 161, Breda Ba 25 (3)
G. 181, Romeo Ro 41 and 41B (8)
G. 201-202, Caproni Ca 97, Ca 101 (2)
G. 203, Dornier Do 23 (6)

This Bü 131 has been modified with an enclosed cockpit and sliding canopy during 1942. The aircraft was camouflaged with Green/Brown uppersurfaces and carried the fuselage code in Red and Yellow Eastern Front markings. (Kovács)

G. 211, Junkers Ju 86 (3)
G. 221, Fw 58K-7, E-l, K-8 (52)
G. 301, Heinkel He 51c (6)
G. 351, Messerschmitt Bf 108B (7)
G. 401, Arado Ar 96A (40)
G. 451, Arado Ar 96B (10)
G. 501, Arado Ar 96A (25)
G. 601, Nardi FN 305 (12)
G. 620, Nardi FN 315 (40)
G. 701, Potez 63 (40)
G. 801, Focke Wulf Fw 58 (22)
G. 901 Arado Ar 96B (35)
H. 001 *Honvèd* (2)

Liaison (*Futár*)

J. 104, Bristol Blenheim Mk I (1)
R. 101, Fieseler Fi 156 (58)

This Bü 131 carried an overall Green camouflage with Yellow theater markings. The aircraft was being used as a liaison aircraft assigned to 102/2 Fast Bomber Squadron (a Me 210Ca-1 unit) during the Summer of 1944. (Punka)

A Hungarian-built Káplár (Corporal) trainer/courier aircraft parked on the grass of a Hungarian airfield. The fuselage code, I.301, was in Red and the fuselage band was Yellow. (Kovács)

A group of young student pilots pose with a Silver painted Fait CR 30 two seat trainer (serial N 0116) at Szombathely airfield. The aircraft in the background is a camouflaged CR 30. (Takács)

This Hungarian-built Levente II courier aircraft nosed over on landing when it hit soft ground, breaking the starboard landing gear leg. The aircraft in the background are WM 21 *Sólyom* (Hawk) short-range reconnaissance biplanes. (Lejtényi)

This CR 30 two seat fighter trainer was Silver dope with Gray panels. The wing struts and landing gear legs were Black. The aircraft in the background is a Romeo Ro 41 which has had its wheel pants removed. (Kovács)

The fuselage code, G6 + 37, on this Nardi Ni 305 trainer was unusual in that the first two digits were outlined in White while the last two were unoutlined. The aircraft carries late style markings and Yellow Eastern Front markings. (Punka)

(Right) G. 125 was a Focke Wulf Fw 56 Stösser trainer. The aircraft was camouflaged and carried Yellow theater marking on the fuselage. The pilot on the right was Vitéz Dezsö Szentgyögyi örm, (Sergeant), Hungary's best known fighter ace. (V. D. Szentgyögyi jr.)

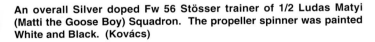

An overall Silver doped Fw 56 Stösser trainer of 1/2 Ludas Matyi (Matti the Goose Boy) Squadron. The propeller spinner was painted White and Black. (Kovács)

This Ro 41 trainer has had its Red fuselage code, G.186, overpainted with Green spots to break up its outline and make it less noticeable. The pilot is using an Italian Salvator type parachute. (Tákacs)

A group of pilots relax next to an overall Silver doped Fw 56 of 1/3 Puma Fighter Squadron. The squadron insignia was Red Puma head with a Red surround. (Punka)

This camouflaged Fw 56 Stôsser was unusual in that it carried a Black fuselage code with White shadow shading. The aircraft was assigned to 1/4 *Dongó* (Bumblebee) Fighter Squadron during the early 1940s. The aircraft was probably used as a liaison aircraft or squadron hack. The propeller spinner appears to be Black and White and the propeller blades appear to be Natural Metal. (Punka)

This was one of tile last Focke Wulf Fw 56s remaining in active Hungarian service. The aircraft was flown by 102 *Richie* (Richie the Dog) Fighter Squadron during 1944. (Punka)

Ground crewmen maneuver an overall Light Gray Arado Ar 96 trainer from its parking spot in the snow at the *Regvi* (pilot school) during 1940. The school was located at Szombathely airfield. The national insignia was carried in six positions and the fuselage code was in Black, (Punka)

This Green/Gray/Brown camouflaged Arado Ar 96 nosed over in the soft ground at Szolnok airfield during the Spring of 1942. From the way the propeller is dug into the earth, the engine was still running when the aircraft went over. The aircraft carries late style insignia and has the fuselage code, G.4 + 24 in Black. (Punka)

A Hungarian Air Force pilot poses with his Arado Ar 96 of the Courier Squadron during the Summer of 1944. The aircraft was camouflaged with Green/Gray/Brown uppersurfaces over Light Gray undersurfaces and carried a Yellow Russian Front fuselage band (which was in a unusual position on the fuselage). (Nagy)

This Dark Green Arado 96 carried the name Sipláda (Hurdy Gurdy) on the nose in White. The aircraft was unusual in that it had a dark colored, probably Black, undersurface camouflage, indicating that it was probably used for night missions over Hungary during late 1944. (Punka)

An overall Light Gray Focke Wulf Fw 58 Weihe with a broken starboard landing gear leg on the forward airfield at Poltava, Russia, during the Summer of 1943. (Terray)

This aircraft was known as the *Meteor-Weihe* and was used for meteorological duties from Budaörs airfield, near Budapest. The Fw 58 suffered a broken starboard landing gear when it became bogged down in the soft earth. The aircraft was overall Light Gray with Black codes. (Kovács)

This Fw 58 was camouflaged in Green/Gray/Brown and was used as a courier aircraft during the Spring of 1944. The aircraft made daily flights between Hungary and the front carrying mail for the troops. (Mészáros)

(Right) This Bf 108 Taifun was painted an overall Dark Blue with a White fuselage code and Yellow Russian Front markings. The aircraft was used as a courier aircraft in Russia during 1943. (Terray)

This Fi 156 Storch (coded R. 1 + 16) of I Courier Squadron was equipped with an under fuselage fuel tank for long range operations over the Russian front during the Summer of 1944. The Yellow theater fuselage band was carried in a non-standard position. (Nagy)

This Fieseler Fi 156 Storch (coded R. 1 + 07) carried the Yellow theater marking in the standard position. The aircraft was active over the Soviet Union during late 1942. (/Kunár)

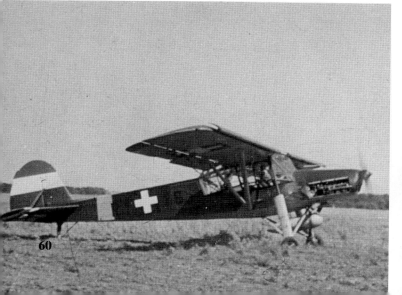

Transports

Originally, Hungary planned that the three Ca 101/2ms purchased during 1930, be used as night bombers instead of transports. These outdated Capronies were replaced by Junkers Ju-86s during 1939,. They were then used, first as paratrooper transports, and later for target towing duties. A total of sixteen Ca 101s served in the RHAF, with the last example being used by the flying school in Szombathely.

The first Savoia Marchetti SM 75 tri-motor transport arrived in Hungary during 1939. It soon became evident that the engines of the aircraft, which had been originally designed as a civilian airliner, were going to be a continuing source of problems. While the engines were undergoing repair at a military facility, the aircraft were converted for use as paratroop transports. Additionally, one aircraft, coded E.105, was modified to carry eight litter and six sitting casualties as a medical evacuation aircraft. This aircraft later crashed near Budapest on its way to the Russian front. The lead aircraft of the paratrooper conversions crashed on take-off on its first military mission due to a hydraulic system failure. Finally, the remaining aircraft were sent back to Italy because of heavy wear and tear.

The Junkers Ju-52 was originally used by *Malért* (Hungarian Airlines) from 1937 on. At the beginning of the war, the three *Malért* aircraft were impressed by the military and additional Ju 52s were ordered from Germany. The Ju 52s were used as tactical transports operating between Hungary and the Russian front. The rights to license-produce the reliable tri-motor aircraft were obtained by the PIRT factory in Budapest and a production line was established. By 1943, three aircraft had been completed, and, in 1944, twenty-seven Hungarian-built Ju 52s left the factory. Because of changing priorities, the company then stopped producing transports and switched to fighter production. Most of the Ju-52s were destroyed by American attacks on the military airfields at Csakvar and Vaszar.

A special Hungarian military delegation traveled to Italy during 1942 to investigate the possibility of utilizing the Fiat G-12 for transport duties. Although an order was placed for fourteen aircraft, only five were actually delivered. At the end of the war, four aircraft were still under construction at Fiat on the Hungarian contract. Although the aircraft performed satisfactorily, they were deployed on only a few occasions. One of them was shot down by American fighters over Pápa on 13 October 1944, another fell into Russian hands, two were blown up on 22 March 1945, and one was destroyed by American bombs at Horthy-liget (on the outskirts of Budapest).

Transport Aircraft Codes:

E. 101, Savoia Marchetti SM 75 (5)
S. 001, Focke Wulf Fw 58 K1/2 (3)
S. 101, Junkers Ju 52 (ex-*Malért* [3])
S. 151, Fait G-12 (5)
S. 201, Junkers Ju 52 (22)
U. 861, Junkers Ju 52 (ex-*Malért* [6])

This Caproni Ca 101/3m was modified with its upper gun deleted for use as a paratroop transport by 1 Ejtöemyös szállitó század (Paratroop Transport Battalion). Even though it was being used as a transport, it still carried its old bomber fuselage code B.I + 13 in Red. bomber codes with red letters. (Takács)

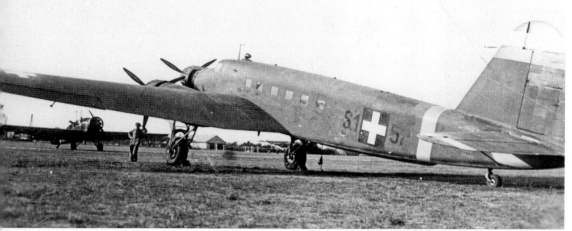

This tri-motor transport was a Fiat G 12. The old Italian markings are visible on the vertical fin and rudder, even though they were overpainted with Hungarian insignia. Of the five G 12s delivered, one was shot down by American fighters on 13 October 1944, another was captured by the Russian, two were blown up on 22 March 1945, and one was destroyed in a bombing raid on Horthy-liget (just outside of Budapest). (Punka)

This tri-motor SM 75 transport, fuselage code E 105, was converted for use as a medical evacuation aircraft and carried Red Crosses on a White disk on the fuselage side. The aircraft conducted a ambulance service between Hungary and the Russian Front during 1942. (Kovács)

This Ju 52 transport was impressed from *Malert* (Hungarian Air Lines). Originally it carried the civil code HA-JUB, before being taken over and given the new code U8 + 62. The aircraft were active over the Russian Front during 1943. Molnár)

A pair of ex-Malert Ju 52 civil transporl aircraft enroute to a forward airfield in Russia during 1943. The aircraft in the foreground carried the fuselage code U8 + 63 (Werk Nr. 5600). (Punka)

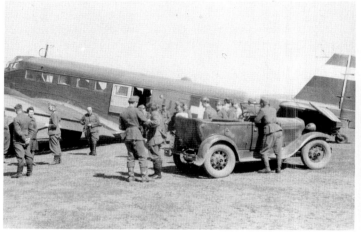

Hungarian Air Force personnel pose with a Hungarian-built Ju 52/3m transport. The aircraft was armed with two MG 15 machine guns in the rear of the cabin and a manually operated turret with a MG 15 machine gun. The Ju 52 was assigned to 102/1 Szállító század (Transport Squadron) during late 1944. (Stifter)

This Focke WulfFw 58KI-2 (ex Malert, civil code HA-FOD) suffered a collapsed landing gear leg. It was unusual in that it carried the fuselage code in Black with a White outline. (Kovács)

Captured Aircraft

During the war, the RHAF put a number of captured aircraft into service. During the Polish campaign, a number of the Polish Air Force aircraft managed to escape to neutral countries, or to countries like Hungary that sympathized with the Polish cause. One Polish aircraft, a PZL P.lla fighter was used by the RHAF as a fighter-trainer and later as a sport plane.

Escaping Polish pilots also flew two RWD 8 liaison aircraft to Hungary. These were used by the RHAF as liaison aircraft and basic trainers. Both aircraft were given Hungarian camouflage and military markings.

During the Slovakian conflict, an Avia B-534 fighter made a forced landing on Györ airfield. The aircraft was repaired and used by as a trainer. From 1943 on, it was used as a tow plane by the Sport Flying Club of the University of Technical Sciences. The aircraft was destroyed at Györ airfield during the evacuation of 1945.

During the Hungarian advance into the Soviet Union, a number of flyable Russian aircraft were captured, most of which were turned over to the Germans. One two-seat UT-2 basic trainer was retained and utilized by the liaison squadron. It was nicknamed *Sanyi* (Alex) by Hungarian flyers.

The first Ilyushin Il-2 was captured during 1942 and given full Hungarian markings. The aircraft was actually rebuilt from two damaged Il-2s and test flown by the RHAF. The aircraft was destroyed during the 1943 Russian winter offensive. A second Il-2 fell into Hungarian hands during early 1945. This aircraft carried Hungarian military markings and national colors, but was not given a fuselage code. It was used to study the results of different fighter attacks and was blown up during the retreat.

American aircraft that were captured by the RHAF carried Hungarian markings; however, their fuselage code consisted of one or two digits numbers.

This PZL P.11a fighter escaped from Poland and was taken on charge by the RHAF with the fuselage code G. 191. It was used as a fighter-trainer for student fighter pilots. (Punka)

This Czech B-534 fighter plane was captured when its pilot made a forced landing on a Hungarian airfield. The aircraft was assigned the fuselage G.1 + 92 and, with its guns removed, was used as a fighter-trainer. (Kovács)

Captured Aircraft Codes

G. 001, UT-2 (1)
G. 191, PZL P11a (1)
G. 192, Avia B-534 (1)
I. 281, RWD-8 (2)

Experimental Aircraft

In 1940, it became clear that, to fulfill all the requirements of the RHAF, the supply of aircraft from abroad would be insufficient and a government run aircraft design office, the Aerotechnical Institute, was established.

The country's general industrial progress had also encompassed the aeronautical industry and the "Jupiter" aero-engine section of the Weiss Manfred factory was capable of developing precision engines for new aircraft designs. Here, an engineer named Gyorgy Jendrassik, developed the prototype of an efficient gas turbine engine. After several hundred hours of testing, he designed a light, 1,000 hp gas turbine for use in an aircraft. The CS-1 type engine consisted of a fifteen-step compressor and a ten-step turbine with an annular burn chamber. A portion of the fuel was used to cool the power turbine. The engine was very efficient. The 13,500 rpm turbine turned a propeller at 3,600 to 1,800 rpm. The design, at the time, was the first of its kind in the world, but because the experiment had taken so long to reach this point, further development of the project was halted.

The first aircraft to be powered with the planned CS-1 engine was the X/H, a twin-engine destroyer which was begun during 1940. The three-men crew (pilot, observer and gunner) were seated above the glass-nosed front section, while the armament and bomb bay were housed inside the fuselage. The aircraft's construction, minus the power plant, was finished in 1942; however, the gas turbine power plants were never completed.

A trainer variant of the X/H, the X/G, was also built. To study the flight characteristics of the design, the aircraft was fitted with two 240 HP Argus AS 10c engines. During 1943, the X/G was flown to Ferihegy airfield, but further development stopped when the Me 210Ca-1 went into production. Both the X/H and X/G were destroyed during an American bombing attack in the Spring of 1944.

The RHAF had a constant shortage of secondary and advanced trainers. Using the WM21 for these purposes was very expensive considering the aircraft's fuel consumption, especially in a country struggling with a fuel shortage.

There were three objectives the design bureau planned to achieve: first, to design trainers with small engines for blind flying and dive

Designed by Professor Varga, the RMI-2 (X/G) prototype was fitted with two AS 411 Argus engines to test the flight characteristics of the design. Tests revealed that the aircraft was capable of a top speed of 223 mph (360 km/h). The wide landing-gear was designed to make take-offs and landings easier and to train pilots selected to fly the Fw-190. (Kovács)

bombing training. Second, to design a modern side-by-side, two-seat fighter trainer and third, to design an advanced trainer for fighter pilots progressing to the Bf 109 fighter.

To meet the first objective the Z/G trainer was developed. The prototype was completed in early 1943, and it was awaiting military trials that would determine if serial production would be undertaken when it was burned in a hangar during an American bombing attack on 13 April 1944.

To achieve the second objective, two variants of the V/G fighter-trainer were constructed. The Argus AS 411 engine powered aircraft were capable of flying at a speed of 223 mph (360 km/h). The wide landing-gear was designed to make take-offs and landings easier and also made the aircraft suitable to retrain pilots on the Fw-190 fighters. The prototypes were awaiting test flights, before commencing serial production, at the end of 1944.

To meet the requirements of the third objective, a mixed wood and metal construction fighter-trainer, the M/G, was built. This small aircraft had the cockpit layout and the landing-gear configuration of the Bf 109 fighter and was capable of flying at a speed of 236 mph (380 km/h). The goal was to provide fighter training on one aircraft from the first take-off to weapons training. This aircraft was destroyed at Ferihegy during a bombing attack.

The tricycle undercarriage concept, spearheaded by the American P-39

Airacobra, started to gain popularity during the 1940s. The Aerodynamics Institute also considered building a small, high speed aircraft utilizing the nose-wheel concept. The *Szunyog* (Mosquito) was a small aircraft capable of 115 mph (250 km/h) and powered by a 45 HP Walter Persy II engine, with the pilot seated in a nearly reclined position. This aircraft, like the others, was destroyed in the Air Force Experimental Institute's hangar at Ferihegy.

In 1944, the fuselage and the wing structure for a twin-engined heavy fighter were built. The twin-boomed, nose-wheeled aircraft was planned to have been powered by both Daimler Benz DB 605 tractor and pusher engines. Its armament included a 30MM engine-mounted cannon (like the Bf 109), two heavy machine guns and a cannon in each of the booms and wing joints. One highlight of the design was the use of an ejection seat. Because the Heinkel-designed ejection seat design was not available, this seat was designed as a "rail car". The seat was propelled upward on two rails by a powerful spring, the force of which was combined with the opening force of the nose-wheel's mass. The mechanism was able to catapult a 220 pound (100 kg) person to height of 13 to 16 feet (4 or 5 meters), high enough to clear the arc of the rear propeller.

At the end of 1940, the only Hungarian designed single-seat fighter, the WM 23 *Ezüst Nyil* (Silver Arrow), was ready for test flying. The WM23 had an elliptical wing and a traditional tail wheel. It was powered by a 1,030 hp WM 14/B engine and was capable of flying at a maximum speed of 329 mph (530 km/h). The aircraft's landing speed was reduced to 100 km/h by the utilization of Flower-flaps. On 21 April 1942, during a test flight, the aircraft experienced aileron-vibration at 9,800 feet (3,000 meters) and the pilot was forced to bail out, leaving the sole prototype to crash. Further development of the WM 23 was halted when the Bf 109 went into production.

Experimental Aircraft Codes

XH-01, RMI-1 (1)
XG-01, RMI-2 (1)
ZG-01, RMI-3 (1)
ZG-02, RMI-4 (1)
      RMI-6 (1)
VG-01, RMI-7 (1)
XV-01, RMI-8 (1)
MG-01, RMI-9 (1)
V-501, Weiss Manfred WM23 (1)

The RMI-3 *Honvéd* (Z/G) prototype dive bomber training aircraft had a very similar cockpit and forward fuselage layout to the Focke Wulf Fw 189. The prototype was completed during 1943, but before it could complete its testing, it was destroyed in a hangar fire on 13 April 1944. (Kovács)